Acknowledgements

We are grateful to the Chartered Institute of Management Accountants for their support in providing funds for this research. We also wish to express our thanks to the directors, partners, managers and staff in TNT, the Peugeot Motor Dealership Network, Eversheds and Arthur Andersen for their generosity regarding the time and resources they put at our disposal. The insights gained and the findings which have resulted from this research would not have been possible without their co-operation and full support. We are grateful, too, for the time and efforts of personnel at a fifth organisation (another mass service) which participated in the research study, but which, on reflection, regrettably decided not to consent to details being published.

The organisations provided a wealth of data, much of which has been reproduced in the exhibits contained within this book. We stress, though, that the views expressed here are those of the authors, and not necessarily those of the organisations studied, or those of the Chartered Institute of Management Accountants.

Contents

Preface

This book aims to give practical guidance to help service managers develop effective measurement systems to monitor and control business performance. The guidance is based on how four successful UK service organisations link strategy and operations through their performance measurement systems. Our premise is that performance measurement is central to control: you get what you measure and what gets measured gets managed.

The four organisations studied are:

- TNT (a mass distributor of parcels);
- the Peugeot Motor Dealership Network (sales and servicing of Peugeot cars);
- Eversheds (a major law firm); *and*
- Arthur Andersen (an international accounting and consultancy firm).

While these four are all for-profit service organisations operating in highly competitive environments, many of the ideas and issues raised and approaches described will be equally relevant to those working in the public sector.

There is a consensus that some form of performance measurement system is an important part of organisational control, but there is no general model that conveys a precise definition of such a system. Organisations pursue their own strategic objectives and operate in different environments with differing technologies, and so will require different measures of performance. However, Professor David Otley has suggested that common to all systems is the need to answer three basic questions:

- What are the dimensions of performance that the organisation is seeking to encourage?
- How are appropriate standards to be set for the measures?
- What are the rewards for achieving these standards?

In Chapter 2 these questions are developed into an organising framework for characterising a performance measurement system. The framework comprises three building blocks that capture a total of twelve separate performance measurement factors. The next four chapters present detailed descriptions of the performance measurement systems adopted within the four case organisations. These are then compared and contrasted in Chapter 7 using the three building blocks framework. This analysis leads to the development of five general factors, common to the four organisations, that seem to represent the basis of best practice in this area.

All the research described in this book was managed and undertaken by Lin Fitzgerald, Lecturer in Management Accounting at the Warwick Business School, University of Warwick and Philip Moon, Senior Lecturer in Management Accounting at the School of Business and Economic Studies, University of Leeds. The empirical data was collected through in-depth interviews combined with an examination of internal documents and the non-participatory observation of company practices, including in some instances company meetings. The interviews were carried out with a range of personnel both at corporate or partnership level and at business unit level, involving nearly 50 individuals in total.

This study extends the previous research study carried out by Lin Fitzgerald, Robert Johnston, Stan Brignall, Rhian Silvestro and Professor Christopher Voss, *Performance Measurement in Service Businesses* (CIMA, 1991), by linking the performance measures set at the strategic, board level with the detailed operational measures that help translate strategy into action.

1
Executive Summary

The aim of this book is to help managers develop effective performance measurement systems to translate strategy into action. Our premise is that performance measurement is central to control, you get what you measure. The core of the book documents and discusses the performance measurement systems adopted by four successful UK service organisations; TNT, the Peugeot Dealership Network, Arthur Andersen and Eversheds.

The key questions addressed are; what *dimensions* of performance should be measured, how are appropriate *standards* set and what *rewards* are associated with achieving the targets? These are the building blocks for performance measurement. All the companies adopt a range of performance measures including profitability and service quality type measures. Setting targets for performance continues to be an area of lively debate within organisations. We found extensive use of internal benchmarking, so that the performance achievements of the 'best' units become the targets for other units, leading to a culture of continuous improvement. Rewards for achievement of performance varied from tangible monthly financial bonuses to the more intangible 'feel good' factor because someone, a customer or a colleague, said 'well done'.

Our view is that there is no single set of performance measures, no single basis for setting standards for those measures and no universal reward mechanism that constitute some perfect performance measurement system, applicable in all contexts. What emerges from our research, however, is the set of five common characteristics below which we suggest represent best practice.

- *Know what you are trying to do* – this must be driven by the corporate strategy.
- *Adopt a range of measures* – financial and non-financial.
- *Extract comparative measures* – there must be a benchmark for performance.

- *Report results regularly* – this discipline promotes knowledge and action.
- *Drive the system from the top* – senior management need to use the system.

Performance Measurement and Control

> *What you measure is what you get. Senior executives understand that their organisation's measurement system strongly affects the behaviour of managers and employees. Executives also understand that traditional financial accounting measures like return-on-investment and earnings-per-share can give misleading signals for continuous improvement and innovation – activities today's competitive environment demands. The traditional financial performance measures worked well for the industrial era, but they are out of step with the skills and competencies companies are trying to master today.*
>
> R S Kaplan and D P Norton (1992)

2.1 Introduction

A central question for management of any organisation is *how well are we doing?*. Considerable time is often devoted by management to developing a mission statement, but translating that statement into a set of integrated performance measures to control, monitor and reward performance which is consistent with the mission has received less attention. The aim of this book is to give practical guidance on how four successful UK service organisations – TNT, the Peugeot Dealership Network, Arthur Andersen and Eversheds – make that crucial link between strategy and operations through the performance measurement system: *making it work*.

Simmonds[1] has coined the expression 'strategic management accounting' being: 'the provision and analysis of management accounting data about a business and its competitors for use in developing and monitoring business strategy'. The monitoring of company performance against those factors that are critical to its gaining and sustaining a competitive advantage should be an important component of any strategic management accounting system. Several frameworks have been proposed that explore the types of performance measures used at this strategic level.[2,3,4] However, for an organisation to be successful these key performance indicators, defined in the language of corporate strategy, need to be translated into some system of performance measures used throughout the whole organisation, recognising that what gets measured gets managed.

In this context, the service sector poses particular problems for performance measurement. Frequently fairly junior personnel are in the front line delivering the service to the customer and with the customer-oriented strategies adopted by many of today's organisations ensuring a consistently high level of service is difficult. The remainder of this chapter explores the nature and types of service businesses and introduces the *dimensions, standards and rewards* framework which is used in Chapter 7 to compare the approaches to performance measurement in the four case companies. This comparison leads to some general observations regarding the methodologies adopted to make performance measurement systems work.

The case studies form Chapters 3 to 6. For each of the case study companies a brief description of the organisation's strategy and the services offered is given to provide the context for the detailed description of the performance measurement system that follows. A commentary is then provided for each case organisation to emphasise the key features that seem to make the system work; that is, the features that drive the organisation's strategy forward. The commentaries include a number of direct quotes from employees at the organisations to substantiate the conclusions reached.

2.2 *The service sector: scope and diversity*

Service industries are those included in sections 6 to 9 of the Standard Industries Classification (SIC) and form a significant proportion of UK economic activity. In 1994 services accounted for 67 per cent of UK Gross Domestic Product (CSO 1995) and this proportion is steadily growing. The sector is diverse, embracing tourism, financial services, retail businesses, healthcare, catering and communications; a common feature being that they treat people or provide goods and services for them.

In a previous study of performance measurement in service businesses three generic types of service organisation were identified: *professional services, service shops* and *mass services*.[2] These archetypes span several standard industry classification sectors and were used to explore the way performance measures and mechanisms varied between the three service types. The case studies in this research provide examples of all three categories: TNT is an example of a *mass service*, the Peugeot Dealership Network represents a *service shop*, while Arthur Andersen and Eversheds are examples of *professional services*. The classification scheme is used here, together with the *dimensions, standards and rewards* framework, developed in section 2.3, to analyse the performance measurement systems of the four case companies.

The classification scheme is presented below together with definitions of the service types. The three service types are differentiated in terms of the number of customers processed by a typical business unit per day against six other classification dimensions:

- people/equipment focus;
- front/back office focus;
- product/process focus;
- level of customisation of the service to any one customer;
- discretion available to front-office staff;
- contact time available with front-office staff.

In this classification scheme (see Figure 2.1) the number of customers processed by a typical unit per day determines the volume of demand placed on the service business. The other six classification dimensions detail aspects of the response to that demand.

Professional services are high-contact services where customers spend a considerable time in the service process. Such services provide high levels of customisation, the process being highly adaptable in meeting individual customer needs. A significant amount of staff time is spent in the front office and contact staff are given considerable discretion in dealing with customers. The provision of professional service tends to be peopled-based rather than equipment-based. Emphasis is placed on the process (how the service is delivered) rather than the product (what is delivered).

Figure 2.1: Service classification scheme

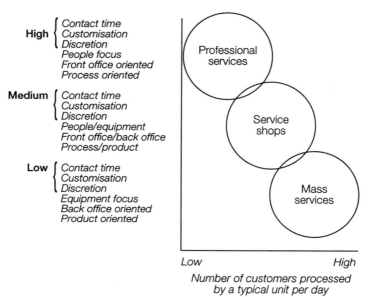

Mass services have many customer transactions, involving limited contact time and little customisation. Such services are predominately equipment-based and product-oriented, with most value added in the back office and restricted discretion available to front office staff. The means-ends relationships are clear; the mainly non-professional staff have a closely defined division of labour and follow set procedures.

Service shops are characterised by levels of customer contact, customisation, volumes of customers and staff discretion, which position them between the extremes of professional and mass services. Service is provided by means of front and back office activities, people and equipment, and of product/process emphasis.

Obviously, not all companies will fit neatly into one exclusive category. Hybrids exist within companies: some business units may fit into the professional category, corporate banking services for example, whereas retail banking may be more closely aligned with a mass service company. In addition, as service strategies change in response to the current and predicted future environment, business units may move from one classification to another. Nevertheless, the kinds of performance measures and mechanisms used will be affected by the type of service unit.

Although service businesses have a wide range of service delivery processes, mixes of inputs and types of output, there is a set of four key characteristics which distinguish them from manufacturing businesses and influence the approaches to control and performance measurement. These characteristics are:

- simultaneity;
- perishability;
- heterogeneity; *and*
- intangibility.[2]

The production and consumption of many services are *simultaneous*; for example, receiving dental treatment or taking a rail trip. The customer has to be there during the process. Most services, therefore, cannot be counted, measured, inspected, tested or verified in advance of sale for subsequent delivery to the customer.

Second, if services cannot be stored, they are perishable. This *perishability* removes the buffer frequently used by manufacturing businesses to cope with fluctuations in demand. Controlling quality and matching supply to demand are, therefore, key management problems in services which are often exacerbated by the presence of the customer during the service delivery process.

Third, many services have a high labour content. Consequently the standard of service may vary, the service outputs are *heterogeneous*. This places particular pressures on the measurement and control systems to try to ensure consistent quality from the same employee from day to day and to get comparability of performance between employees.

Finally, most service outputs, unlike manufacturing outputs, are *intangible*. For example, when buying consultancy services there are tangible measures of performance such as the completion of the project on schedule, but other less tangible factors such as the helpfulness and responsiveness of the staff which influence the overall level of customer satisfaction. Identifying what the customer values from the complex mix of tangible goods and intangible services makes the process difficult to control. Output measures such as the number of bed-days in a hospital do not necessarily capture the service provided or the benefits experienced by customers.

These four characteristics pose extra strains on service managers in terms of identifying what to measure and, in particular, when and how to measure performance.

2.3 *Three central questions*

- What should be measured?
- How are standards set for the measures?
- What are the rewards for achieving the targets?

This section integrates existing ideas to develop a framework for reviewing how an organisation uses its performance measurement system to translate strategy into action. There is broad agreement that some form of performance measurement system is an important component of organisational control, and furthermore, that there is no general model that conveys a precise constitution of such a system. Different organisations will be pursuing different strategic objectives, operating in different environments with different technologies, and so will require different performance measures. However, *Otley*[5] suggests that common to all systems is the need to answer three basic questions, which can be viewed as forming the basic building blocks of a performance measurement system.

1. What are the *dimensions* of performance that the organisation is seeking to encourage?
2. How are appropriate *standards* to be set?
3. What *rewards* and/or penalties are to be associated with the achievement of performance targets?

These three building blocks capture a total of twelve separate performance measurement factors which are shown in Figure 2.2 and which are discussed below.

Figure 2.2: The dimensions/standards/rewards building blocks for performance measurement systems

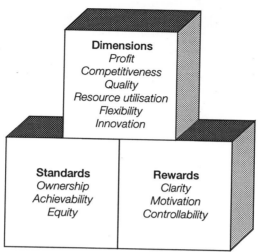

2.3.1 Dimensions

There is increased recognition that companies compete on a wide range of dimensions whose evaluation cannot be confined to narrow financial indicators. Simply focusing on financial performance can give misleading signals for the continuous improvement demanded by today's competitive environment. Important issues of customer satisfaction and establishing good employee relations would be missed by such a system. The challenge is to develop non-financial performance measures which capture the quality, service and flexibility issues of today's customer-oriented competitive strategies.

Common threads emerging from a review of three performance measurement frameworks – *Fitzgerald et al.'s* determinants and results matrix[2], *Kaplan and Norton's* balanced scorecard[3] and *Lynch and Cross's* performance pyramid[4] – are that performance measures should:

- be linked to corporate strategy;
- include external (customer service type) as well as internal measures;
- include non-financial as well as financial measures; *and*
- make explicit the trade-offs between the various measures of performance.

In addition both the balanced scorecard and determinants and results frameworks distinguish between 'results' of action taken and the 'drivers' or 'determinants' of future performance (see Figures 2.3 and 2.4). The balanced scorecard complements 'financial measures with operational measures on customer satisfaction, internal processes, and the organisation's innovation and improvement activities that are the drivers of future financial performance'.[3] The *Fitzgerald et al.* framework proposes that measures of financial performance and competitiveness are the 'results' of actions previously taken and reflect the success of the chosen strategy. The remaining four dimensions of quality, resource utilisation, flexibility and innovation are factors that determine competitive success, now and in the future. They represent the means or 'determinants' of competitive success. This is an attempt to address the 'short-termism' criticism frequently levelled at financially focused reports. It emphasises the notion that improvements in quality, for example, may not hit the bottom line in the current period but if these quality improvements are valued by customers future financial results should reflect this.

Figure 2.3: The balanced scorecard

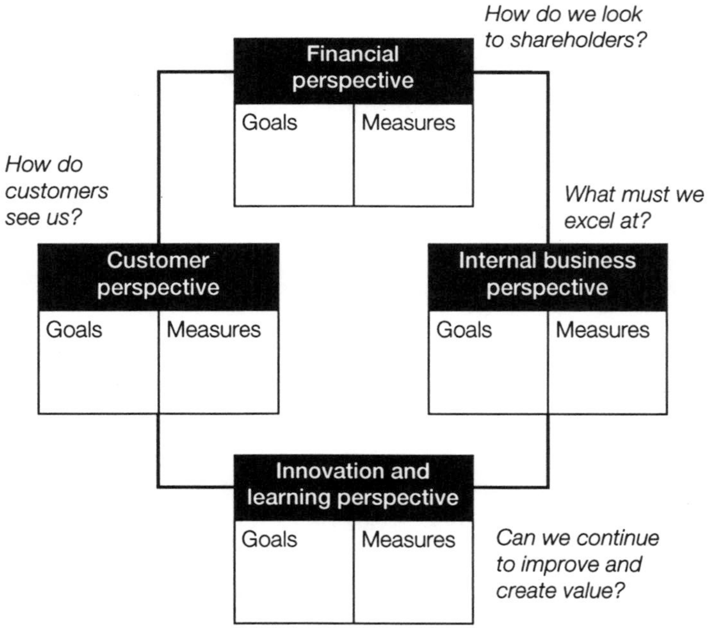

Figure 2.4 *The results and determinants framework*

	Dimensions of performance	Types of measure
RESULTS	Competitiveness	Relative market share and position Sales growth Measures of the customer base
	Financial	Profitability Liquidity Capital structure Market ratios
DETERMINANTS	Service quality	Reliability Responsiveness Aesthetics/appearance Cleanliness/tidiness Comfort Friendliness Communication Courtesy Competence Access Availability Security
	Flexibility	Volume flexibility Delivery speed flexibility Specification flexibility
	Resource utilisation	Productivity Efficiency
	Innovation	Performance of the innovation process Performance of individual innovations

An important feature of the three frameworks reviewed is that they are prescriptive in the sense that the dimensions of performance are specified, e.g. customer perspective and quality. However, actual measures of these dimensions will depend on the business type and, importantly, on the specific competitive strategy adopted by the organisation. That is, the types of measures used need to reflect, either directly or indirectly, the success factors that are critical to the achievement of corporate strategy.

2.3.2 Standards

The second building block relates to the setting of expected standards once the actual dimensions and measures have been selected. This involves consideration of who sets the standards (*ownership*), at what level the standards are set (*achievability*) and whether the standards facilitate comparison across the business units (*equity*).

Ownership

In establishing targets, the importance of individuals being responsible for owning the standards has long been established: this is often facilitated by the adoption of a budgetary system based on employee participation[6,7]. This is considered to be beneficial to the organisation as it alleviates, or at least reduces, many of the dysfunctional consequences associated with traditional control models. In particular, managers who participate in the standard-setting process are more likely to accept the standards set,[8] feel less job-related tension and have better relationships with their superiors and colleagues.[9] Participation does, however, provide opportunities for introducing budgetary slack.[8]

Achievability

Research findings indicate that defined quantitative targets motivate higher levels of performance than if no targets are set[10] and, providing the target is accepted, the more demanding the target the better the resulting performance.[11,12] Thus the budget level that motivates the best performance is unlikely to be achieved all of the time and adverse budget variances will occur. If adverse variances are treated punitively by management this may encourage budgetary slack,[13] where individual managers overstate expected costs and/or understate expected revenues, so that subsequent monitoring of actual outcomes presents them with a favourable evaluation.[14] Budgets need to be realistic enough to encourage employees to perform, but not set at levels so high they become totally demotivated. Finding the balance between what the company views as achievable and what the employee views as achievable is a frequent source of conflict.

Equity

Are the targets comparable across all similar business units, or do some have an inherent advantage unconnected with their own deliberate initiatives? For example, some business units may be subject to higher degrees of environmental uncertainty than others. *Govindarajan* found empirically that the higher the level of uncertainty, the greater the reliance placed on subjective judgement in appraising performance, with less reliance on objective, financial data.[15] It would be inappropriate and inequitable to treat the two extremes in the same way.

2.3.3 Rewards

The third building block relates to the reward structure of the overall performance measurement system. It is concerned with guiding individuals to work towards the standards derived above. It means posing three questions. First, does the system exhibit *clarity* to all those whom the system effects? Second, if you know what is expected of you how are you *motivated* to achieve that performance? Third, what level of *controllability* do you have over areas for which you are held responsible?

Clarity

If one of the main purposes of the performance measurement system is to ensure the successful implementation of company strategy then this should be clearly understood by employees throughout the organisational structure. Research studies indicate that most managers react well to clear, unambiguous targets,[16] and acceptance of targets is facilitated by good upward communication.[11] People should know what the organisation is trying to achieve, what is expected of them, and exactly how and why their own contribution, to the organisation's performance in meeting its objectives, will be appraised.

Motivation

In principle, employees may be motivated to work together for the pursuit of the company's strategic objectives by tying performance-related rewards, for example bonuses, to the attainment of key success factors. Goal clarity and participation have been shown to contribute to higher levels of motivation to meet targets, providing managers accept those targets.[11] However, the effects of targets on motivation are complicated by the reward system and how it is used. Is the system used positively to encourage, or negatively to condemn, or both? When properly used, a responsibility accounting system does not emphasise blame. If managers feel they are criticised and rebuked when unfavourable variances occur, they are unlikely to respond in a positive way. Instead, they will tend to undermine the system and view it with scepticism.[17]

Controllability

The traditional view in responsibility accounting is that people should only be made responsible for financial elements which they can control (that is, have some influence over) and that they should only be rewarded for results of their efforts. The implication is that managers would lose interest in cost control if their performance was being judged on events outside their control. From the viewpoint of the organisation as a whole all costs are controllable and need to be controlled. The difficulty here is in pin-pointing responsibility, particularly regarding the allocation of those costs arising from activities that benefit many departments or divisions within an organisation. Inevitably, the principle of cost controllability also involves the principle of the perceived fairness of cost allocations.

Evidence from field studies tends to refute the controllability principle described above. Both *Merchant*[18] and *Otley*[19] found managers were held accountable, to varying degrees, for events and results over which they did not have complete control. The focus of evaluation was on how managers responded to events for the benefit of the business.

2.4 Conclusions

The service sector is diverse and is an important part of the UK economy. The characteristics of the sector present particular problems in control and measurement for service sector managers. The dominance of customer-oriented strategies and the increasingly competitive environment faced by organisations demands that a range of performance dimensions are measured and linked to the corporate strategy of the company. This range of dimensions forms the first building block of a performance measurement system. Consideration also needs to be given to how targets are set for these measures and what systems of reward structures are used for achievement of targets.

In the next four chapters we present case studies corresponding to four large UK service organisations representing a cross-section of service archetypes. One organisation, TNT (Chapter 3), is a mass service, one, the Peugeot Dealership Network (Chapter 4), is a service shop, while the remaining two, Eversheds (Chapter 5) and Arthur Andersen (Chapter 6), are professional services. Finally, in Chapter 7, the research findings from the individual cases are synthesised using the *dimensions/standards/rewards* model developed above as a unifying framework. This leads to some general observations regarding the methodologies adopted to make performance measurement systems work.

References

1　Simmonds, K., 'Strategic management accounting', *Management Accounting*, (ICMA), April, pp 26-29 (1981).

2　Fitzgerald, L., Johnston, R., Brignall, S., Silvestro, R. and Voss, C., *Performance Measurement in Service Businesses*, CIMA (1991).

3　Kaplan, R.S., and Norton D.P., 'The balanced scorecard – measures that drive performance', *Harvard Business Review*, January – February, pp 71-79 (1992).

4　Lynch R.L., and Cross, K.F., *Measure up! Yardsticks for continuous improvements*, Blackwell (1991).

5　Otley, D., *Accounting control and organisational behaviour*, Heinemann (1987).

6　Argyris, C., *The Impact of Budgets on People*, New York, Ithaca (1952).

7　Becker, S., and Green, D., 'Budgeting and employee behaviour', *The Journal of Business*, October, pp 392-402 (1962).

8   Emmanuel, C., Otley, D., and Merchant, K., *Accounting for Management Control*, Chapman and Hall, 2nd edition (1990).

9   Hopwood, A., 'An empirical study of the role of accounting data in performance evaluation', *Journal of Accounting Research* (supplement), 10, pp 156-182 (1972).

10 Tosi, H., 'The human effects of managerial budgeting systems', in Livingstone, J. (ed.), *Management Accounting: The Behavioural Foundations*, Grid. Columbus, Ohio (1975).

11 Hofstede, G.H., *The Game of Budget Control*, Tavistock (1968).

12 Chow, C.W., 'The effects of job standards, tightness and compensation schemes on performance: an exploration of linkages', *The Accounting Review*, pp 667-685 (1983).

13 Cyert, R.M., and March, J.G., *A Behavioural Theory of the Firm*, Prentice-Hall (1963).

14 Ezzamel, M., and Hart, H., *Advanced Management Accounting: An Organisational Emphasis*, Cassell (1987).

15 Govindarajan, V., 'Appropriateness of accounting data in performance evaluation: an empirical evaluation of environmental uncertainty as an intervening variable', *Accounting, Organizations and Society*, 2, pp 125-135 (1984).

16 Kenis, I., 'Effects of budgetary goal characteristics on managerial attitudes and performance', *The Accounting Review*, 54, pp 707-721 (1979).

17 Hilton, R.W., *Managerial Accounting*, McGraw-Hill (1994).

18 Merchant, K. A., 'How and why firms disregard the controllability problem', in Burns & Kaplan (eds), *Accounting and Management Field Study Perspectives*, Harvard Business School Press (1987).

19 Otley, D., 'Issues in accountability and control: some observations from a study of colliery accountability in the British Coal Corporation', *Management Accounting Research*, June, pp 101-123 (1990).

TNT is a dynamic international group principally engaged in freight transportation with a growth record worldwide that is impressive by any standards. Since its formation in Australia in 1946, TNT has developed into one of the largest and most flexible transport organisations in the world, established in 190 countries, employing more than 52,000 people and operating a fleet of 350 planes and 24,000 vehicles from over 3,000 terminals worldwide.

TNT delivery services brochure, 1994

3.1 Introduction

TNT was first established in the UK in 1978, and now approximately one-seventh of its worldwide workforce is employed here, where it enjoys a market lead in the overnight distribution of parcels. The bulk of TNT's UK operation is through TNT Express (UK) Ltd. This company has three principal divisions: *TNT Express Delivery Services*, offering a comprehensive range of nationwide door-to-door express delivery services; *TNT Logistics*, providing dedicated distribution solutions tailored to specific customers' needs; and *TNT Newsfast*, specialising in distribution for the newspaper and magazine publishing industries. In addition, there is a centralised management and administration function which services all three divisions.

The focus of this chapter is restricted to TNT Express Delivery Services. Business is broken down in two different ways: first by division, that is by type of business (e.g. Supamail, Sameday ...); and second by depot, that is, by the location of the business. Each depot will offer all, or most of, the different divisional services. Our research concentrates primarily on the depot structure.

The top-level service provided by TNT Express Delivery Services, and consequently the most expensive, is the *next day before 9.00a.m.* service, cheaper variants including *next day before 10.30a.m.*, *next day before noon*, and *next day (time unspecified)*. Thus, an Oxford business person who leaves an important package in a Torquay hotel bedroom on a Tuesday afternoon can have it delivered before the start of the next working day directly to his or her home address.

The critical success factor for TNT is to deliver the goods to the right place at the right time. If marketing claim at the point of sale that a delivery is possible, then operations need to ensure that the delivery actually takes place at the required time and place. Reliability is essential. Success in this area is dependent on a carefully planned operational system and a smooth operational flow. Fundamental to successful, reliable delivery is the extent of TNT's geographical coverage of the UK, and hence its number of potential customers. This is dependent on the number, size and location of the depots. Currently, all services are available throughout the UK with some exceptions: for instance, the premier *next day before 9.00a.m.* service is not available in some of the more remote parts of Scotland, Wales and Cornwall (in common with all other national carriers).

The operational system adopted is structured like a giant wheel, with a central hub and a set of spokes (motorways and major trunk roads) running between the hub and the outer rim. On this outer rim are 28 depots, situated strategically around the country as shown in Figure 3.1. Each of these depots has a clearly defined, non-overlapping territory, so that the whole of the UK is broken-up across the 28 responsibility centres, thereby ensuring nationwide coverage as far as possible. The central hub is in the Midlands at Atherstone, approximately twenty miles north of Birmingham and close to several motorway junctions. Recently, a second, smaller hub was opened in Croydon to cater for the growing volume of London-specific freight.

Each weekday, each depot is responsible for the co-ordination and collection of all packages that customers in their territory wish to send. These are sorted at the depot, those for delivery in the same territory being retained separately. The remainder are packed into large trailers (trunks) which are then driven to the hub at Atherstone. Depots may send anything from one to ten trunks each night, with arrival times at the hub, and therefore departure times from the depots, co-ordinated centrally in an extensive computerised scheduling exercise. On arrival at Atherstone the trunks are unloaded, again according to strictly controlled schedules, and packages are mechanically sorted by destination on purpose-built conveyors. The reverse process then takes place with trunks being loaded with packages for delivery to the depot in a particular region,

Figure 3.1: The location of TNT depots in the UK (December 1993)

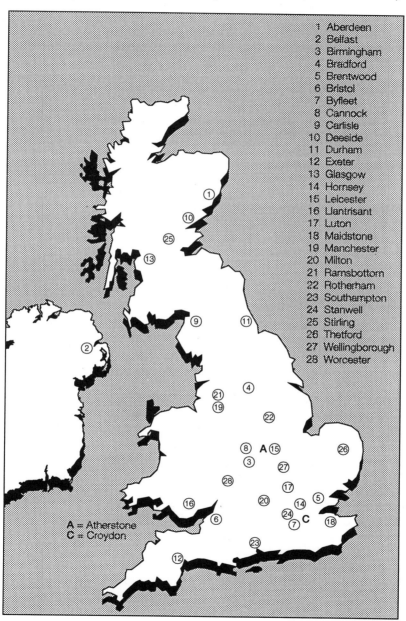

1 Aberdeen
2 Belfast
3 Birmingham
4 Bradford
5 Brentwood
6 Bristol
7 Byfleet
8 Cannock
9 Carlisle
10 Deeside
11 Durham
12 Exeter
13 Glasgow
14 Hornsey
15 Leicester
16 Llantrisant
17 Luton
18 Maidstone
19 Manchester
20 Milton
21 Ramsbottom
22 Rotherham
23 Southampton
24 Stanwell
25 Stirling
26 Thetford
27 Wellingborough
28 Worcester

A = Atherstone
C = Croydon

where they are again unloaded, and the packages sorted into appropriate delivery rounds in time for the 9.00 a.m. deadline. Referring back to the earlier example, the Oxford business person's important package would actually travel from Torquay to Exeter to Atherstone and to Milton before finding its way to the home address in Oxford.

Responsibility for the smooth running of this system falls on the general manager for network operations at the hub, and on the 28 depot management teams at the rim. There is an additional management layer comprising five divisional general managers, but this layer is more concerned with the sales and marketing of the services than with operations. At each depot a depot general manager is employed, who has overall responsibility for sales, operations and administration. It is the depot general manager who, together with his local management team, effectively control the fortunes of the organisation, and whose actions will determine how near TNT come to achieving the strategic objectives of profitability and growth via coverage and reliability.

3.2 The performance measurement system

At the corporate level, TNT's mission can be stated succinctly as being the number one express parcel delivery service in the UK. Sustaining such a market position has obvious implications for profitability and growth and these are monitored regularly at board level through an analysis of the management accounts against targets. Profitability and growth, though, are the results of success rather than the determinants. Critical to being successful is the quality of service offered: are packages delivered to the right place at the right time? Customers will be quick to change their allegiance if reliability is questionable. Accordingly, a key performance indicator measured on a weekly basis is the overall 'delivery-on-time' performance; the number of consignments delivered on time expressed as a percentage of the total number of consignments booked. The actual performance level achieved is compared with the prior week's performance and with the current company target. TNT perceives that the key to improved performance at the depots is for the hub to be operating effectively. As a result, the company monitors the 'end-of-sort-time' on a daily basis against a predetermined target in the early hours of the morning (around 3.00 a.m.). Updated predictions are made throughout the night to act as an early warning system as even a short delay beyond the target end-of-sort time can be potentially costly for TNT. This is due to consequent money-back guarantees or the need for some depots to employ sub-contractors to meet the delivery deadlines.

At the depot level, four separate performance measurement mechanisms are used. Although each one carries implications for the other three, there is no formalised connection made. The four relate to:

(i)   the depot overall;
(ii) sales and customer care;
(iii) deliveries; *and*
(iv) finance and administration.

3.2.1 *The depot overall*

The need to generate profit at the company level is driven down directly to the depots, a weekly profit and loss account being produced for each depot. Each week the 'ladies and gentlemen' memorandum from the managing director, is sent out to all depot general managers. This memorandum (an example of which is reproduced as Figure 3.2) focuses exclusively on the revenue and profits earned by individual depots, these being displayed in the form of 'league tables' in order of actual profits achieved for that quarter. Specific mention is made of the top profit-makers for the week, and all managers earning in excess of budgeted profits for their depot.

The detailed profit and loss statement produced weekly for each depot shows its results for each week in that quarter, and the cumulative actual against budget. In this context, profit is the difference between actual revenues achieved for that week less the costs incurred. The revenue for any given depot relates to all sales in that territory for that week; in other words, the revenue represents the total value of all consignments *collected* by the depot, regardless of their ultimate destination. TNT deliberately does not attempt to allocate this revenue on some common basis between the collecting and delivering depots. Costs comprise the depot operating costs (wages and salaries, sub-contractor costs etc.) and allocated costs. There are three types of allocated costs; group services (a recharge of centralised administration expenditure), divisional overheads, and central operating costs (for example, the costs of operating the hub).

Bonuses for the depot management team can be earned quarterly on

Figure 3.2: The 'ladies and gentlemen' report

PRIVATE AND CONFIDENTIAL ADDRESSEE ONLY

From: Tom Bell   Ref: TB/JRO/6528
To: General Managers   Date: October 29, 1993

Ladies and Gentlemen

Week 16 Results
Week 16 continued the run of disappointing results with a revenue beating performance but costs far exceeding acceptable levels as we fail to achieve the return on revenue of   %.

	Week 16		**Weeks 14-16**	
	Budget £000	**Actual** £000	**Budget** £000	**Actual** £000
Revenue				
Profit (loss)				
Profit as a % of revenue				

The top six profit makers in week 16 were as follows:

	Week 16 **Profit**	**Week 16** **Profit as %** **of revenue**
Milton		
Wellingborough		
Luton		
Deeside		
Hornsey		
Southampton		

"Remember it's your commitment that counts"

Continued opposite...

October 29, 1993

Martin   tops the list of the leading profit makers for the week with an excellent result just ahead of the cumulative league leader Louis   . The remaining
members of the top six are very closely grouped with Tom   featuring in third
spot ahead of Ron   , Dawn   and Geoff

Martin   heads a list of only ten budget beaters for the week. This is far
below the strike rate required for the company to reach its weekly target.
There were some excellent performances from Dawn   , Bill   , Brian
and Jim   to name but a few, however the majority of depots have failed to
reach budget by quite some margin.

Depot General Managers achieving better than budget profits for week 16
were:

	Week 16 Profit £000	Week 16 Profit better than budget by £000
Milton		
Hornsey		
Birmingham		
Stirling		
Ramsbottom		
Deeside		
Wellingborough		
Worcester		
Rotherham		
Glasgow		

We must give urgent attention to improving margins. It is therefore imperative
that the price increase effective October 25 is sold positively to all customers
and that the cost reduction programme is implemented with no deterioration
in service. The successful implementation of this strategy will give the required
profit performances.

Regards

Tom Bell

the basis of target profit levels. Achievement of the target or better, within a quarter, leads to financial bonuses of a fixed sum plus a small proportion of profits above budget for the depot general manager, with a similar bonus being paid to the depot management team. A successful depot general manager can earn bonuses equivalent to 25 per cent of salary.

3.2.2 *Sales and customer care*

The transference of corporate sales objectives for growth to divisions, depots and sales employees is simple. All concerned are encouraged to maximise sales revenue in accordance with nationally set price schedules dependent on size, weight, distance and location. Sales quality is rigorously monitored and, except for high-volume customers, the company operates a no-discount sales policy. Sales targets are agreed for divisions and depots and actual performance is rewarded on a commission basis, although this is not adjusted for delays in collectability of the debt or for debts that remain uncollectable. In addition to standard commissions, bonus prizes are awarded for those employees exhibiting outstanding sales performance. Further incentives are available for sales leads initiated by non-sales staff such as drivers who are actively encouraged to seek leads while carrying out deliveries. Similarly, though again at the discretion of individual depots, employees (usually drivers) can earn commissions based on the first four weeks' revenue from new Truck-Care (the TNT vehicular maintenance operation at each depot) customers introduced by them. Overall sales performance is reported and monitored in weekly league tables.

As part of its overall marketing strategy, TNT Express Delivery Services has adopted a formal customer care programme, for which it has gained awards from the Motor Transport industrial sector. Its commitment to customer care statement is represented by Figure 3.3. Performance against this standard is monitored regularly, partly on an informal basis, partly as a by-product of other parts of the performance measurement system, and partly by 'random' comprehensive checks. For example, external organisations are employed to research TNT's performance by sending consignments through the system. This tests out TNT's claims that they will 'answer your incoming telephone calls promptly, courteously and within six rings', that the parcel will be properly collected, weighed, labelled and delivered, that invoicing will be clear and easily understood, and any queries dealt with efficiently.

Figure 3.3: The TNT customer care statement

Our Commitment
to Customer Care.

- We will answer your incoming telephone calls promptly, courteously and within six rings.
- When calling you will always be able to speak directly with the TNT person you ask for, irrespective of seniority and without having to state your name, your company or the reason for your call.
- A team of one field sales person and one telephone sales person dedicated to a defined post-code area will be made personally responsible for the day-to-day handling of your account. This enables us to establish a sound business relationship and provide you with unparalleled levels of sales and after sales service.
- As a TNT Express customer, you will be contacted on a regular basis at least once every six weeks to ensure that we maintain a close liaison and provide excellence in customer care.
- Should we ever fail to collect your consignment as agreed, we will ensure delivery is made meeting your original time criteria wherever possible, at no extra cost to you.
- We pledge to check your collected consignments against their consignment documentation and to verify the number of items, their weight, destination, selected service level and postcode. We will then ensure that all your parcels are accurately routed and delivered on time.
- In the unlikely event that we misdirect one of your parcels, we guarantee to deliver the item direct within the shortest possible time at no extra cost to you.
- We will provide instant access confirmation of delivery information 24 hours a day, 365 days a year via our automatic telephone response system – TNT Tracker. Personal confirmation of delivery is available immediately on request the next working day.
- TNT Express invoicing will always be clear and easily understood. Any query you may have regarding invoicing or accounts will be quickly and efficiently resolved. All enquiries will be responded to immediately.
- Our reputation for safe and secure handling enables us to offer Free Transit Liability cover of up to £15,000 per consignment with confidence, providing extra peace of mind for you.
- In the unlikely event that you have to make a claim, we guarantee that a written response will be forwarded to you within 24 hours and, if necessary, a full investigation will be undertaken to resolve any claim.
- We will communicate with you regularly to ensure that you are fully informed of our developments and to seek your opinion on the services we provide, our people and our standards.
- All TNT employees are our ambassadors and they are trained to be efficient, helpful and courteous at all times. Despite the rarity of complaints, we guarantee that should you ever complain about the behaviour, attitude or road manner of any TNT person, the issue will be taken up and we will reply to you within 24 hours.

CUSTOMER CARE AWARD
WINNER

Tom Bell
Managing Director, TNT Express Delivery Services

Note as well from the customer care statement that TNT Express customers 'will be contacted on a regular basis at least once every six weeks to ensure that (TNT) maintain a close liaison ...'. Sales staff are expected to follow this through accordingly.

3.2.3 *Deliveries*

The fact that delivery performance is perceived to be fundamental to the success of TNT has already been discussed. This is recognised in the operational performance measurement system, the key report of which is the weekly 7-star service performance report. The layout of this report for week 22 is shown as Table 3.1. In keeping with other TNT Express systems, this is set out in the form of a league table, ranked in order of delivery-on-time performance. This is the first of the seven indicators included. The others are the proportion of 'failures' (where the whole system has broken down for a particular consignment), the proportion of deliveries that result in credit notes or that are unmatched with invoices, the proportion of misroutes, the number of late trunks (that is, trunks arriving late at the hub and, therefore, potentially delaying the end of sort time), and the amounts of loss claims and damage claims expressed as a percent of revenue. Further weekly reports are circulated that present more detailed analysis about each of the categories above. A standard target is set for each of the seven indicators; for instance the company-wide target for the number of late trunks is zero. Any depot achieving the target or better across all categories would gain a 7-star rating for that week.

Under the incentive scheme adopted, until early 1993, depots achieving a 5-star rating across the first five categories would earn a bonus to be shared out among the depot operations team (headed by the depot and operations managers). A further bonus would be earned for reaching this standard over five consecutive weeks.

While the 7-star service report continues to be the key performance measurement tool for deliveries, the bonus scheme is now based on delivery-on-time performance only, the actual percentage achieved being compared with a depot specific, regularly monitored and updated, target. Meeting this standard on average over a four-week period earns a fixed bonus for the depot manager and a further bonus to be shared out across the team.

Poor performance on delivery does not only impact personal bonuses, it also leads to adverse profit and loss account charges. Each depot is

Week 22 Targets	% del on time	Failures	% dels on c/notes & unmatched	Misroutes	Late trunks	Loss claims as a % of revenue	Damage claims as a % of revenue	Star rating
Brentwood								
Birmingham								
Exeter								
Ramsbottom								
Southampton								
Leicester								
Manchester								
Byfleet								
Milton								
Bradford								
Worcester								
Stirling								
Croydon								
Wellingborough								
Rotherham								
Deeside								
Stanwell								
Bristol								
Cannock								
Carlisle								
Aberdeen								
Glasgow								
Thetford								
Luton								
Durham								
Llantrisant								
Maidstone								
Hornsey								
Belfast								

charged for any loss and damage claims for which it is responsible, it has to foot the bill for sub-contractors hired as a result of misroutes, and will be fined £500 for each trunk that is late on arrival at the hub (unless there are mitigating circumstances outside the depots' or drivers' control, such as a major accident on the motorway).

3.2.4 *Finance and administration*

In addition to sales and operations, the finance and administration function is also crucial to TNT's success. The monitoring and evaluation process involves the circulation of regular league tables, detailing the finance and administration performance for each depot, on a monthly basis. These reports focus on the level of outstanding sales ledger balances, the volume of credit notes issued and the speed with which invoice queries are dealt with. Thus, there are reports ordered by debtors weeks, and by the percentage of debt over 60 days old. The measures are summarised in the 'five fives' monthly incentive scheme report, the layout of which is shown in Table 3.2.

Incentives are based on achieving targets across each of the four categories, that is, the number of debtor weeks, the proportion of debt over 60 days, the proportion of invoice queries, and the value of credit notes raised relative to revenue in total. The standard scheme rewards performance within the 'five fives' is shown in Table 3.3.

A fixed bonus is available to share out across the finance and administration section at the depot, though the basis of the allocation of this bonus is at the discretion of the managers concerned. Tougher targets are the '54321' scheme and the 'bullseye', with bonuses increasing accordingly. In September, eight depots achieved five fives, five achieved 54321, while one depot – Exeter – gained a bullseye. A further, substantial bonus is paid to the finance and administration manager if, during the course of the year, the depot gains four bullseyes or 24 points, calculated in accordance with the detail in Table 3.3.

Table 5.2 The plot plots finance and administration report

Key:
* Depot achieved five fives
** Depot achieved 54321
*B Depot achieved bullseye

| | | | | Queries received as a % of inv. raised | Value of credits as a % of revenue |
| Targets → | | 5.5 | 5% | 5% | 0.5% |
Depot	Responsibility of:	Debtor weeks	60-day, %	Invoice queries	Credit notes
Byfleet		5.6	2.3	1.6	.3
Milton		5.1	4.5	1.9	.4 *
Bristol		5.4	.0	2.4	.2 **
Maidstone		5.8	3.2	2.2	.5
Wellingborough		5.8	1.5	2.2	.5 *
Southampton		5.5	1.6	1.4	.5
Stirling		5.4	.0	.2	.1 **
Worcester		5.2	1.8	2.0	.3 *
Brentwood		5.8	1.7	1.4	.8
Rotherham		5.8	2.6	2.4	.4
Ramsbottom		5.4	.2	1.3	.2 **
Exeter		4.9	.0	2.5	.2 *B
Llantrisant		5.3	3.3	1.6	.4 *
Hornsey		6.3	3.0	2.7	.7
Cannock		5.5	.2	1.1	.2 *
Digbeth		5.7	2.5	1.3	.2
Belfast		5.7	2.3	1.7	.6
Aberdeen		6.0	3.9	2.6	.5
Luton		4.9	.2	1.1	.1 **
Thetford		5.5	.9	.5	.5 *
Durham		6.0	1.7	2.9	.3
Leicester		6.1	4.3	1.5	.8
Carlisle		5.4	.5	.7	.1 **
Glasgow		6.2	2.9	.8	.3
Bradford		5.4	2.8	1.8	.5 *
Deeside		5.5	4.2	1.4	.3 *
Manchester		6.2	6.4	2.6	1.7
Stanwell		5.8	1.6	4.5	.8

Table 3.3: Finance and administration incentive scheme targets

	Five fives	54321	Bullseye
Debtor weeks	5.5	5.4	5.0
Proportion of 60-day debt	5%	1%	0%
Queries received as % of invoices received	5%	3%	3%
Value of credits as % of revenue	0.5%	0.2%	0.2%
Points contribution towards annual bonus	1	3	5

3.3 *Commentary*

In this section we appraise the performance measurement system at TNT in terms of:

- the dimensions of performance measured within the organisation;
- the way in which standards are set; *and*
- the reward mechanisms that are used to encourage employees to meet and exceed these standards.

3.3.1 *Dimensions*

It is clear that TNT Express utilise a wide range of performance measures. Although each depot is assessed overall on the basis of a single indicator, net profit, different functions within the organisation and within each depot are measured on a whole range of indicators, specific to the area of responsibility. Most of the measures are hard, formal measures. This raises an interesting research question: if a greater emphasis is placed on achieving such objective, measured targets, then as these targets become more and more challenging to meet, might they start to take over as a primary concern, at the expense of more intangible parts of the service process? For instance, the 'what the customers say about us' file of letters maintained in the reception at the hub, reveals the potential importance of the drivers in building up customer relations. This is not just referring to the physical delivery of the service on time, but also to the manner of the delivery – the driver's politeness and friendliness, and a general attitude that conveys that the driver has time to communicate with the specific customer, before rushing off to the next one. The network operations general manager, reinforces this by pointing out:

> *It's not actually the sales people that have most contact with the customer, it's actually our drivers, ... and we spend all this money on training sales people, but we don't really spend that much money on our drivers at all. ... Syd or Joe who comes everyday and is cheerful and helps them out when they've got a bit of a problem, and doesn't mind staying for an extra ten minutes or helping them to pack or whatever it happens to be, is worth their weight in gold.*

At TNT a key impact of the customer care programme is the reinforcement of the need to be concerned for the customer, and so a balance is achieved between the hard, profitability-related measures and the softer, customer-related ones.

A related concern is that the use of performance measures directly relevant to specific functions might lead to an over functional approach, i.e. an individual's attention is constantly drawn to his or her own set of indicators, therefore issues may be seen from a departmental viewpoint rather than from a company-wide viewpoint. This is only too apparent to head office management; as the network operations general manager states:

> *We are organised very strongly on functional lines which has served us extremely well, ... And what that does, of course, is ... in each area of the business we do achieve functional excellence ... so I don't want to knock it; it's a very powerful weapon within the organisation that there is technical quality whether it's on finance or administration or sales or operations ... we are very strongly focused on improvement, constant improvement, and we measure ourselves to death in league table format on a weekly basis in order to make sure that the standards are adhered to and improved upon ...*

> *But I have a feeling that as you move forward and as you become technically better in each area of your function, that technical or functional excellence becomes less important. Because what you're trying to do is to differentiate yourself from the competition, which I think you can only do by really making sure that you are not only listening to the different functional voices within the organisation, but reacting to what the customer really wants.*

To some extent, the use of net profit as an overall performance measure for each depot pushes the responsibility for cross-functional awareness very clearly in the direction of the depot general managers.

3.3.2 Standards

Ownership

While operating performance standards are imposed from the top, the depot budgets are prepared by the depots and presented at formal review meetings for approval or revision. Central control is very tight, and once established, actions at a depot that require additional funds would need to pass through several authorisation stages. For instance, if a depot was swamped with a high administrative workload, a case for a further member of staff (even a temporary one) would need to be sanctioned by the finance and administration manager at the depot, the depot general manager, the regional general manager, and finally the network operations general manager. The central staffing policy is that the latter signs everything. The justification for this level of central control comes directly from the performance measurement system.

> *I believe that that benchmarking exercise we did proved that at a local site you haven't got all the information ... you don't realise you're actually over staffed because that's the way things have been done for ever. Centrally you take a view that you can do direct comparisons. We proved the point on one occasion where this depot, which was exactly the same size ... [as another depot] ... had got four people less in that area, yet was very successful.*

Achievability

Although the company adopts a policy of continuous improvement, individuals need to feel that the performance targets are achievable. In general, many standards were seen as reasonable by the depot general managers. Thus, for example, the 7-star and five-fives systems were well understood and accepted; however, opinion on the overall targets agreed for each depot for profit and delivery performance was less favourable. Several personnel expressed negative views in this area; for example,

> *In a number of instances the revenue target set for [Milton] by head office is just a fairy story … we can't keep growing at the same rate for ever.*

Further, the achievability of certain targets was seen as being effected by several factors outside the control of those responsible. For instance, regarding the achievement of the delivery on time target:

> *the benchmark is unfair due [partly] to the book-in system. Argos and Sainsbury cause delays since they want to know in advance when it's coming [to fit in with their own goods inward schedule] … they won't accept it from any old driver just turning up.*

Similar sources of grievance in this context were misroutes, situations where goods never arrived, and situations where the drivers were on time, but there was nobody around to accept delivery.

Equity

Some depots have inherent advantages because of their location near to areas of high distribution activity. For example, Milton and Wellingborough depots both collect high volumes of consignments on a daily basis from one or two large contracts. While any customer/supplier relationships must be cultivated and maintained, the existence of the contracts would not necessarily have been as a result of the depot's own actions. These two depots, however, are always high up in the league tables (see Figure 3.2), and usually win many of the sales awards. Similarly, Birmingham and Cannock depots are both very near the Atherstone hub. Neither, then, should (or do) have many, if any, late trunks, and both are expected to exhibit excellent delivery-on-time performance, compared with, say, the Carlisle depot which is over 200 miles away.

Perhaps surprisingly, the general view here was 'good luck to them', especially following the introduction of the new incentive system for delivery performance based on specific targets for each depot. In any event, depots are held responsible for their own performance wherever their location. No depot (with the possible exception of Belfast) is seen as a special case, and it is not acceptable for any depot to consistently operate at a loss.

3.3.3 Rewards

Clarity

Individuals in particular functions were well aware of the mechanisms of the performance measures that affected them directly. Nor were they under any illusions about the TNT requirement for performance, and that the performance standards have to be achieved if not regularly, then at least occasionally. Again, this clarity of focus is evident from some of the earlier quotes, for instance the network operations general manager's comments on functional excellence. Individuals were generally aware of the kind of measures used in other functional areas, although knowledge regarding detail was more limited.

Motivation

On the positive side, the TNT performance measurement system is seen as providing evidence of capability, and as recognising successful initiatives. Most individuals, in all areas of the depots, wanted to see their department rising in the league tables, and felt great satisfaction when they did so. The linked financial incentives were also seen as helpful, but, in some cases, becoming less tangible as targets are systematically made more difficult. The flip side for the depots is that poor performance is also transparent. Every other depot will know when you have failed to meet standards, and when your own league table position is deteriorating. As one depot general manager put it:

> *There is nothing worse than being in charge of a depot that loses money. Every Tom, Dick and Harry looks at the league tables. There is tremendous pressure to make profits.*

In addition to this, most depot personnel interviewed were aware that their own workloads had increased substantially over the last few years. The volume of consignments collected and delivered had increased at a faster rate than staffing levels. Long hours seemed to be becoming the norm for many, and stress levels were higher. While the performance measurement system was not directly responsible for this, it was seen as implicated to some extent, as it provided the data for head office benchmarking of the kind described above.

Controllability

The issue of controllability gives rise to certain conflicts. These fall into one of three specific areas; allocated costs, the matching of costs and revenues, and inter-functional disputes. The first of these reflects the well-established antagonism of any division towards its head office on being charged large sums of money as its share of head office costs. At TNT there are three types of allocated cost; group service costs, divisional overheads and central operating costs. In so far as the latter two relate to observable processes (e.g. the hub), the associated costs are (grudgingly) accepted. It is the group service costs (typically around 9 per cent of revenue) that cause most complaint. Although standard allocation bases do exist for these costs, some depot managers do not feel they are adequately communicated.

The head office view on group service costs can be encapsulated by the finance director's statement that: 'the weekly P & L has to be accurate to be of value'. At the depot level, while it is appreciated that group service costs are real costs that need to be covered by the profits from the depots, the managers interviewed seemed unaware of the exact basis for their allocation. For example, 'we have no idea what it [group service cost] is going to be from one week to another', and 'we seem to get penalised for being successful', reflecting the relationship between the size of revenue and the amount allocated. The consequent disgruntlement might be mitigated to some extent through more precise communication and/or a simplified system, comprising a weekly fixed charge, plus a weekly variable charge dependent on one or two key cost drivers, such as the number of consignments or the number of trunks. While this would give rise to periodic adjustments for under- or over-recoveries, such amounts would be relatively small, and therefore easier for managers to accept. The company's view, however, is that the existing allocation system is satisfactory as it ensures that managers are aware of the full costs of running the business.

Second, it was discussed earlier how revenue from a consignment is credited entirely to the collecting depot, even though the costs of delivering it are met by the destination depot. The depot has control over the sales, and hence revenue, generated by its area, and control over the delivery of consignments from sales generated by other areas. Thus, the costs and benefits associated with each consignment are not matched together at the depot level. This has implications that need to be considered when appraising the true profitability of each depot. Operating statistics consistently show that some depots always collect far more than they deliver, while others deliver far more than they collect, simply as a function of geographical location.

Third, the system can lead employees to focus their attention on their own role rather than on the process as a whole. This can lead to conflicts with other functions within the organisation, or even within the same depot. For instance, one depot manager described how:

> *Sales somewhere can gain a great contract that adds £600 to their revenue, but it's inconvenient for me to deliver because the delivery location is in the middle of nowhere ... yet I'm the one who gets stuck with the £50 cost to use a sub-contractor.*

While this was (rightly or wrongly) seen as balancing out in the long run, it was nonetheless a source of frustration whenever it happened. Similarly, the following observation was from an F & A manager:

> *Sales keep selling to a customer that is a slow payer [i.e. greater than the finance target of 5.5 weeks], but I can't tell them to back off.*

For the company as a whole both positions would be defensible. TNT would not necessarily want to turn away sales, but there is a clear need to encourage customers to pay within a reasonable time. Consequently, it is left to each depot to resolve conflicts such as this as best they can. The issue is that these conflicts become more prevalent as a result of adopting a performance measurement system that is predominantly functionally based.

3.4 Discussion and conclusions

As discussed earlier, TNT aims to retain its position as the number one express parcel delivery service in the UK. This means that the organisation requires sustained profitability and growth, and to achieve this needs to offer a high-quality service. In particular, the company has to ensure that it delivers the right goods at the right time to the right place. At the corporate level this mission is clear, but how exactly has the performance measurement system been used by management to push the strategic direction of the organisation into all aspects of the operational side of the business? At TNT there seem to be five properties of the system which have facilitated this process. The first three of these relate to the dimensions, standards and rewards framework, namely measuring the right things, internal benchmarking, and reward mechanisms. The two additional properties of the system are the use of league tables and the presence of a corporate champion. These are each discussed below.

3.4.1 *Measuring the right things*

At TNT, the content of the performance measurement system, in terms of the strategy adopted and the translation of that strategy into a range of performance measures, is well understood and clearly communicated throughout the organisation. The specific measures used cover a range of dimensions designed to focus the organisation on factors thought to be central to corporate success, and not restricted to traditional financial measures. Key issues are translated into detailed action plans so that every individual is aware of their role and its requirements. For example, one of the quality of service measures included in the customer care programme is to answer the telephone within six rings. Individuals are left in no doubt as to what to do. Everyone within the organisation (interviewed) has a clear idea about what TNT is trying to do, and what the key factors are that will enable it to do so; 'get the service level right' came up repeatedly as being the single most important objective. The specific sets of (functional) performance measures also echoed different aspects of TNT's corporate strategy. For example, operations' measures have a clear focus on deliveries-on-time, sales' measures on volumes achieved.

The comprehensive system of performance measurement at TNT, and the ways in which performance on some dimensions is communicated to employees, operates very formally. However, we found evidence of an effective informal communication network, particularly between the depots. The members of the depot management team seemed to spend a substantial amount of their time on the telephone to managers at other depots. This was partly to sort out queries relating, for instance, to undelivered packages or incorrect addresses. There was an acceptance that mistakes did occasionally happen, but rather than cause high degrees of resentment because one depot's performance might be adversely impacted by another depot's mistake, there was a 'swings and roundabouts' kind of attitude; an expectation that over time things would even themselves out. Regarding mistakes that are made, where a pattern becomes apparent acceptance quickly becomes strained, with more assertive action being taken. Inter-depot communication is also an important mechanism for sharing innovations across the company such as the way that particular aspects of sales or operations could be performed. Generally, relationships between the depots seemed to be particularly strong within the regions, where there are more convenient opportunities to arrange regular meetings.

3.4.2 Internal benchmarking

Internal benchmarking is used at TNT to provide sets of absolute standards that all depots are expected to attain. There is a continual drive towards best practice, and central management is quite prepared to highlight one depot's strong performance in one area as justification for not excusing another's inferior performance in the same area. Benchmarks on delivery performance re-emphasise quality of service, while benchmarks on profitability re-emphasise the need to make money. As one senior manager pointed out:

> *Exeter make money despite having a small business area, and being a long distance from the hub.*

So then, it is argued, can any other depot.

Where there are differences in what constitutes acceptable, expected performance at individual depots, the setting of standards at TNT is consistent with a budget constrained style of management. However, the level of participation in setting budgetary targets is questionable, and their achievability is perceived as often being extremely difficult. Again though, this would be countered by arguments (hard for depots to refute) that the company has to be continually improving to maintain its market lead over its competition, and that if one depot can achieve a target once, it and other depots can do so again.

Paradoxically, while the success of its continual improvement strategy has been one of TNT's key strengths, it can also constitute a threat. At the time of the study (during the busy pre-Christmas period), the central hub at Atherstone had been operating at virtual capacity levels for several weeks and so the end-of-sort-time had been adversely, though not severely, impacted. This could impose a constraint on the growth of the business as the more reliable the service becomes, the more customers will want to use it, and as more pressure is put on the hub sort, it may become longer and longer, leading to late deliveries and therefore a decline in reliability. The company's strategic plan included the provision of additional central sortation capacity opening in 1994.

3.4.3 *Reward mechanisms*

Incentive schemes are used throughout the business, linking the achievement of company targets with financial rewards. Each functional area at the depots has its own standard, purpose designed bonus scheme which focuses on the key performance indicators for that function, while the depot management team can supplement their earnings further should their depot exceed its targeted level of absolute profits.

For the depot management team our impression was that the profit bonus did act as a powerful motivator, but there was a clear recognition that the profits achieved were the *results* of success not the *determinants*. As such, the day-to-day focus of management is on sales, operations and debt collection rather than on the bottom line. For the functions within the depot, the size of the actual bonus payouts are relatively small. However, there can be very positive non-financial benefits in terms of rewarding teamwork. Achieving a bullseye (finance and administration) or seven stars (delivery) is something to be regarded in high esteem, especially as all other depots are immediately aware of it via the league table reports.

3.4.4 *League tables*

A central feature of the performance measurement system at TNT is the widespread use of league tables that display each depot's performance relative to one another. These emphasise the company's critical success factors of profitability and quality of service by reporting results weekly at the depot level. Implicitly, competition, in terms of performance, is actively encouraged between the depots. An individual's position in the league table is keenly observed both by that individual and his (her) peers. In theory, performance is transparent. In practice, although each depot performs essentially the same function and is measured in the same way, their circumstances may be very different. Some may be near to the hub, some may be far away; some may be located in areas with high collections, some in areas with high deliveries, some in urban zones with well developed road networks, some in remote, rural places. Measuring performance via the league tables makes no allowance for these relative differences; inequity is built into the system.

Further, depot managers and depot personnel are held responsible for areas over which they have no formal control. The network nature of the business implies that there is a high interdependence of depots; the collecting depot will not necessarily be the delivering depot. Business may be generated for which the collecting depot receives the revenue, which is in fact difficult to deliver, but the delivering depot bears the cost. This impacts on both depots' profit statements. The formal system does not recognise such difficulties, the corporate view being that 'the business needs to be managed'; the depots should, therefore, see any such anomalies as mild constraints to work around rather than barriers to break down. Consequently, the delivering depot will discuss the problems informally with the collecting depot. These informal discussions are facilitated by the close communications between depots recognising the interdependencies of the business.

3.4.5 *Corporate champion*

Finally, there is a constant, almost evangelical driving down of the corporate message from the centre, and in particular from the managing director. Head office believes in the performance measurement system and attaches great importance to the results that the system computes. The managing director visits each depot at least once per year, specifically to analyse that depot's performance line by line. Each week his 'ladies and gentlemen' report is awaited by the depot managers to see how well they have performed, both absolutely and relative to other depots, and who has been singled out for special mention.

This strong corporate drive has led to the emergence within TNT of a common ideology – the need to 'get the service level right'. Almost all personnel interviewed mentioned this as an overriding need, and could see how their own roles, whether in management, sales, operations, or finance and administration, assist with this objective. As a consequence, it is generally welcomed that performance reports are received frequently, and show the results for all depots, as this 'reporting structure provides the context, comparisons and the big picture.'

At head office level, 'getting the service level right' also means that there is no market for excuses. The customer is always right. As the network operations general manager says:

there's no point in me telling a customer who's dissatisfied with us that, 'look, we met our service specifications', if he thinks we haven't. That happens quite a lot ... we, for example, have got a before 12 delivery for today and we haven't delivered before 12. Why? Because his customer wouldn't accept it; he wants us to phone first of all and arrange a time to have it delivered in. Now our customer is not particularly interested in why we couldn't deliver before 12, because he's paid us to deliver it before 12.

Now that's been quite a big change that we've had in the last three years on operations in that we have tried to get people away from this defensive, internally focused functional thing. ..What I'm interested in is the gap ... between the deliveries on time in total and 100% ... and all the different reasons why we didn't do that, to our customer, ... [are] as much a failure as us being in an accident, however justified they are. The trouble is you see, that if you allow people to justify it you'll have any number of good reasons why you didn't do things. If you're just absolutely unforgiving and say, 'I'm sorry, ... [I'm] going to be completely unreasonable, I don't accept there are any reasons why you shouldn't deliver on time', then it starts to change their mentality.

Thus, the performance measurement system at TNT reinforces the corporate culture or set of shared values that ensures the continuity and consistency of that strategy.

At TNT all of these five properties have been important in developing a performance measurement system that facilitates the translation of strategy into action: measuring the right things, internal benchmarking, reward mechanisms, the use of league tables and the existence of a strong corporate champion.

In the next three chapters the performance measurement systems used within three further UK service organisations are described. As we shall see, the five key properties at TNT in driving forward company strategy are not necessarily critical in alternative business environments.

4
Peugeot

The outlook for the UK car market looks to be relatively stable with perhaps the hope of some modest growth, the continuation of a lack of growth in the retail market being offset by continued growth in the fleet markets. However, the market will remain extremely competitive and difficult. We look forward to launching the Peugeot 806 multi-purpose vehicles into the UK later this year and continuing to expand the sales of our newer models.

Peugeot Talbot Motor Company plc,
Report & Accounts 1994

4.1 Industry background

The European Motor Industry is characterised by an oversupply of vehicles. Although a single European market exists, with approximately twelve million new car registrations per year, in reality this is complicated by tremendous national interest in terms of national employment pressures, coupled with degrees of government involvement with the industry varying from strong links to part-ownership. The over capacity problem is exacerbated by Korean imports, which now account for approximately 2 per cent of the European market, increasing competition from third world countries plus internally within Europe, Japanese transplants.

Total new car registrations in the UK for 1994 were 1.91 million. The UK car industry, however, has a cyclical nature as shown in Figure 4.1. Within these sales the fiercely competitive fleet market (defined as vehicles being sold to operatives of 25 or more vehicles) has expanded its share of the market from 30 per cent in 1988 to 45 per cent in 1994.

The principal volume manufacturers of cars in the UK are Ford, Vauxhall, Rover, Peugeot, Nissan, Toyota and Honda. Ford has maintained market leadership in the UK over the ten-year period to 1994 and market shares for 1994. Currently Peugeot, the subject of this chapter, lies in fourth place, as shown in Figure 4.2.

Figure 4.1: Total car sales in the UK

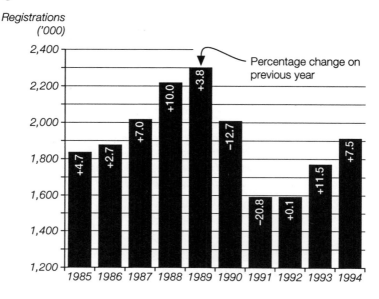

Figure 4.2: 1994 market share

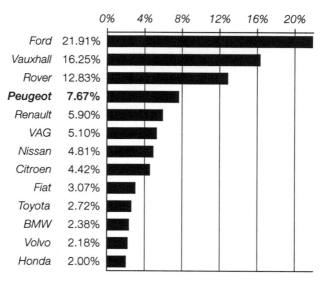

Peugeot's share of the UK market has shown continuous growth over the ten-year period to 1993 when market share was 8.02 per cent (see Figure 4.3). Record UK sales for Peugeot in 1994 amounting to 146,551 registrations were not enough to maintain this continuous growth in market share which fell, slightly, to 7.67 per cent.

Figure 4.3: Peugeot market share

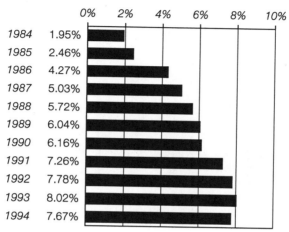

The market place for new cars is under pressure from the over supply. In addition, the quality of new cars in terms of increased mechanical reliability of component life and the tendency to extend service intervals from 6,000 to 9,000 miles (for petrol powered cars), implies the level of opportunity in after-sales service and repairs is reducing. This results in a highly competitive market place for the range of services provided by the Peugeot dealership network.

The Peugeot Talbot Motor Company plc

The Peugeot Talbot Motor Company plc is engaged in the manufacture, assembly and distribution of motor vehicles, replacement parts and accessories in the UK. The content of the Company's Charter for 1994 is shown in Figure 4.4. In the charter there are clear commitments to:

- long-term market share growth;
- improving customer service;
- the provision of secure and rewarding jobs for all employees; *and*

- the provision of adequate profits for the company.

Customer satisfaction is the top priority. There is recognition that competitors are improving performance all the time and that 'the greatest danger we face is complacency'.

Figure 4.4: The company charter

The Peugeot Talbot Motor Company plc
THE COMPANY CHARTER
A broad statement of our objectives

OUR PARTICIPATION AS PART OF THE PSA GROUP
As part of PSA Peugeot Citroen the Peugeot Talbot Motor Company must work within the framework of the overall policies and objectives of the group. Our function is essentially threefold:

1. To play our part in the group's production activities through the operation of our UK plants.
2. To support the group's drive to increase sales worldwide and to become Europe's leading car producer.
3. To help increase the group's profitability to a level that is at least on a par with the best of our international competitors.

OUR COMPANY AIMS
In the UK our principal objectives are:

- To run our production plants efficiently with maximum attention to improving quality and productivity.
- To achieve our annual sales targets for the UK market and to achieve long-term market share growth.
- To provide an outstanding and comprehensive service to our customers.

And, as a result:

- To provide secure and rewarding jobs for our people and adequate profits for the company.

All divisions of the company and all employees have their part to play in the achievement of these objectives. All of us are equally concerned with the subjects covered below.

OUR PEOPLE

Nothing is more important in a company than the motivation and commitment of its employees. We must be positive if we are to succeed.

Our company, therefore, places great emphasis on its policies involving people. As well as providing decent pay and conditions, these policies seek to ensure that employees are properly trained, are treated with respect, are listened to, and are kept informed. The policies aim also to encourage employees as individuals and as members of a team to suggest methods of improving the quality and effectiveness of the work they do.

The principles of 'continuous improvement' in all aspects of our business operations must become part of our normal way of life.

In these ways our working lives can become more satisfying, the company's performance better and the prospects of a prosperous future more secure.

OUR CUSTOMERS AND SUPPLIERS

Customer satisfaction is our number one priority. But to give the concept of customer satisfaction the right emphasis we have to redefine what we mean by the terms. 'Customers' are not only our dealers and the people who buy and drive our vehicles but also those colleagues within the company to whom we 'supply' a service. In this sense we are all 'customers' and 'suppliers'. In short, we are all interdependent. All departments should be precise, quick and efficient in dealing with their 'customers' whether inside or outside the company.

OUR COSTS

Throughout the company costs must be controlled and continually reduced. We must aim:

- To make our products and provide our services right first time. Any form of rework worsens quality and costs money.
- To use plant and equipment properly. Breakdown affects quality and adds to costs.
- To see that the supply of components to production lines and elsewhere in the company is smooth, but that stocks are kept down to 'just-in-time' levels. This point applies equally to finished cars held by the company or by dealers. Excess stocks of any kind cost money.
- To control our commercial and administrative expenses rigorously.

THE FUTURE
The greatest danger we face is complacency. Our competitors are improving their performance all the time. We do not necessarily have to work harder but we must aim to do things more efficiently. We have to look at our business intelligently, always searching for ways to improve on the various matters with which all of us deal. We must question traditionally accepted practices and attitudes; and we must be flexible. We must keep up with technical developments, be progressive and innovative.

Above all, we have to remember that if as a team we can make steady, consistent improvements then the progress of recent years can be sustained and our job security strengthened.

4.2 *The Peugeot dealership network*

This chapter focuses on the Peugeot dealership network in the UK. Peugeot has approximately 400 franchised dealerships in operation in the UK located to provide geographical coverage. Each dealership franchise deals exclusively with Peugeot providing a full range of services covering the sales of new and used cars, car servicing and parts provision. A large proportion of the franchises are privately owned, family run businesses. Stringent conditions are enforced (by Peugeot) on the franchisees in terms of corporate identity and the standards of service offered, from the number and range of demonstrator cars held to the colour of the door handles in the showroom. In return Peugeot provide a wide range of business support such as periodic reviews of the industry and Peugeot's own position within the industry, as well as specific advice for individual dealerships.

Strategy for the dealership network

The long-term sales policy of the company is for continued growth in market share overall while maintaining the market leadership for diesel cars. The plan is to achieve this by building reputation and customer loyalty, specifically:

- building loyalty to the Peugeot marque;
- improving the profitability of dealers;
- improving the way dealers treat customers and prospective customers;
- reducing the costs of distribution and bureaucracy.

Dealer performance is keenly monitored and a wide range of support services are available. In terms of after-sales activities the objective is to continuously improve the services to dealers; for example providing improved technical support through computer-based diagnostic aids and continuing emphasis on training master technicians.

4.3 Performance measurement systems and rewards

Three, separate, formal performance measurement systems are used to monitor dealer performance:

(i) the annual sales plan focusing on the volume of new car sales;
(ii) the 'composite' which focuses on financial results; *and*
(iii) the 'Lion Standards' programme where the focus is on the service quality provided by the dealership.

4.3.1 The annual sales plan

Every dealership negotiates an annual sales plan for new cars with their Peugeot regional office. There are tensions in the negotiation process: while Peugeot want to see ever-increasing sales, the dealers are keen to have realistic targets because achievement of the plan is linked to rewards. A league table report is issued, on a regional basis, naming dealers and ranking them in order of their sales achievement, measured as the percentage of sales achieved compared with the previously agreed targets.

4.3.2 The composite

The *composite* provides a variety of management accounting information drawn from dealership returns and sources external to Peugeot such as the vehicle licensing centre (which provides details of new car registrations by postcode area). Although participation in the composite system by dealerships is voluntary, participation levels have increased over the development period of the system as more and more dealers became convinced of its value. At present approximately 85 per cent of franchisees participate in the system, which is supplied free of charge to dealers. An interesting feature of the system is that although it was devised and developed by Peugeot

in conjunction with Alison Associates it is administered solely by
Alison Associates. Initially, individual dealership information was
held on a completely confidential basis with only summary statistics
being produced. Now the Peugeot national business management
manager and regional directors have authorisation from all dealers to
draw off individual dealership reports, if required.

Three sets of reports are generated from the composite system all
with restricted distribution. The top layer report is a national
summary produced for senior management within Peugeot; each
report is individually addressed and the circulation list is strictly
controlled on a need to know basis. A pro forma for the first page of
the national summary report is shown in Figure 4.5; the commentary
is written by the national business management manager, followed
by key statistics and graphical representation of selected data. The
remainder of the report gives further analysis of the business
segments. Average results are shown, but individual dealerships are
not identified. Considerable effort has gone into the design of the
report in terms of both information content and layout; for example, a
strict discipline is placed on the length of the commentary by the size
of the box.

The second tier of reporting comprises summaries provided to
Peugeot regional managers, each manager only receiving the results
for his own region. Regional managers are the front line contact with
the dealerships: they make visits and maintain close contact with the
dealerships for which they are responsible. They have a range of
information to draw on, seeing the role of their version of the
composite as being to 'confirm what they already know is going on'.

The most detailed reports are the individual dealer composites which
all dealers participating in the scheme receive monthly. These reports
provide information on the individual dealership plus comparisons
with both the 'average dealer' and the 'average of the top 25 per cent
of dealers' performance. To assist the comparison dealerships are
banded into four groups, as shown in Table 4.1, defined by size in
terms of the annual number of new car sales. A dealership will receive
information only on the group within which he operates.

Figure 4.5: National summary

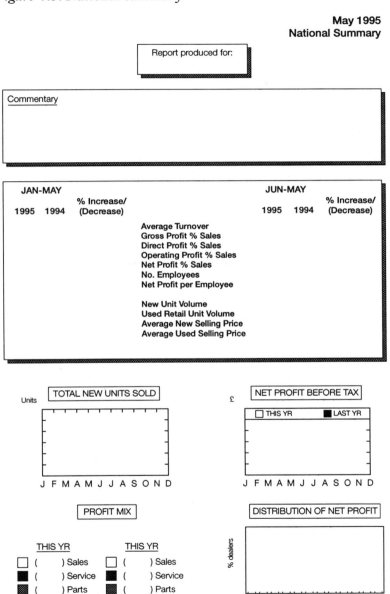

Table 4.1 Dealership groups

Annual number of new car sales	Group
0 – 249	1
250 – 499	2
500 – 999	3
1,000 +	4

The first page of the monthly dealership report contains a short national commentary, provided by Peugeot's national business management manager, and an overview of the individual dealership profitability and market share. This system provides information on sales and profitabilities within each of the four departments of the dealership; vehicle sales, service department, parts department and 'other' departments which includes forecourt and rentals if applicable. As one dealer commented:

> *it gives you all the statistics to help you understand where your bottom line profit is coming from … the comparisons are particularly useful*

4.3.3 Lion Standards programme

Peugeot has been operating its Lion Standards programme for ten years, several changes and refinements having been made over that period. The programme focuses on the service quality provided by the dealership. Its stated objective, printed on all the Lion Standards documentation, is:

> *To develop the volume growth and profitability of the Peugeot dealer network. This to be encouraged by rewarding, through contribution to profit, the achievement of annual sales plan and provision of the highest levels of customer care and operating standards.*

Within the programme there are three areas of assessment:

* entry requirements;
* operating standards;
* Peugeot customer assessment.

Detailed information on each area of assessment and how it will be assessed is provided to all dealers. The programme is directly linked with significant financial rewards and the prestigious 'gold lion award' for an elite group of 50 dealers who produce outstanding performance against the customer assessment plan.

There are distinct bonuses and assessment processes for each of the areas of assessment. As shown in Table 4.2 the highest weighting is given to the customer assessment area of the programme. This represents a major change from the early days of the programme where the focus was on regional staff review of the facilities provided at the dealership.

Table 4.2: Lion Standards assessment areas

Assessment area	Proportion of bonus (1995 programme)	Assessment process
Entry requirements	20%	Central monitoring
Operating standards	20%	Regional staff
Customer assessment	60%	Customer questionnaires Customer complaints Mystery shoppers

Entry requirements

Eligibility to the programme is dependent on the fulfilment of a set of entry requirements. The 1995 programme identifies fourteen factors for assessment including:

- *Exclusivity* – the dealer has to provide exclusive representation for the Peugeot franchise at the approved trading location.
- *Corporate identity* – only approved Peugeot franchise signs may be displayed and the corporate identity standards must be met in all communications media.
- *Demonstrators* – the dealer must run a range of cars in line with the annual sales plan; these cars to be kept clean, well presented and displayed at all times in a signed dedicated demonstrator parking area.
- *Diagnostic capability* – a master technician must be employed throughout the year and be supported by having the latest Peugeot diagnostic equipment.

- *Peugeot experience programme* – every dealer must attend one of the half-day briefing sessions/introductions to the programme.

This section is assessed on a pass or fail basis. Fulfilment of the fourteen factors in this area of assessment, a pass, has two tangible outcomes: first, a bonus is paid – a fixed amount based on the number of new car registrations – and second, the dealership becomes eligible to enter the other two areas of assessment within the programme, operating standards and Peugeot customer assessment.

Operating standards

This section of the programme is designed to measure the extent to which the dealership meets standards which are considered to be 'fundamental to achieving profitable volume growth within the Peugeot franchise'. The assessment is carried out by staff from the regional office. Seventy-one factors are considered in the assessment, each one having a maximum points score. The assessment is comprehensive covering the sales department, the after sales department and the overall management of the dealership. For example, two factors assessed under the sales department are:

- Follow-up letters to customers and prospects are despatched at regular intervals, based upon the date of purchase or contact. Thank you letters to all customers are despatched within five days of purchase and followed up by direct (telephone or visit) sales staff contact.
- All internal and external areas of the sales department are painted and furnished to corporate standard.

Dealers know the areas of assessment and points allocated to each factor score in advance (there are changes in the detail of questions and points allocated from year to year) and receive a full breakdown of their results. In addition an executive summary is provided (see Figure 4.6) showing the dealer score for the Lion Standards programme, the maximum points available, and hence the percentage score achieved by the dealership. Two comparisons are provided; first, the national average point scores achieved by all Peugeot dealers, and second, a comparison of dealerships of similar size, using the same groupings as the composite.

Figure 4.6: Operating standards – executive summary

LION STANDARDS
STATUS REPORT END JUNE 1995
EXECUTIVE SUMMARY

Dealer 10001 ABC Motors Ltd
Region 0 District 0
Guild League 4 56 Dealers

	Your Score	Points Available	% Achieved	Nat. Ave. Points	National Quartile Position
ENTRY REQUIREMENTS	PASS / FAIL				
OPERATING STANDARDS					
Sales Department					
Sales Marketing	xx	xx	xx	xx	xx
Sales Management	xx	xx	xx	xx	xx
Aftersales					
Service Marketing and Management	xx	xx	xx	xx	xx
Parts Marketing and Management	xx	xx	xx	xx	xx
Management					
Business Management	xx	xx	xx	xx	xx
Organisation & Development	xx	xx	xx	xx	xx
TOTAL OPERATING STANDARDS	xx	xx	xx	xx	xx

Customer assessment

The customer assessment section concentrates on customer care issues by measuring the extent to which a dealership meets the expectations of its existing and prospective customers. This assessment is a continuous process measuring the 'Peugeot experience provided by the dealership'. Measurement is by customer questionnaire (administered centrally by Peugeot), mystery shopping, and the central monitoring of customer complaints and complaint response time. This variety of assessment methods is designed to overcome the potential bias associated with only one style of assessment. Figure 4.7 gives a summary of the areas covered and comparisons provided.

The Guild of Gold Lion Dealers

Every year an elite group of 50 dealers are awarded annual membership of the 'Guild of Gold Lion Dealers'. Membership requires outstanding performance against customer assessment and achievement of the annual sales plan. Members are invited to a 'prestigious event' and the results are published in a league table format. Dealerships are assessed in their relevant 'leagues', defined by new car sales. Dealers receive personalised copies of the league table results, the format being shown in Figure 4.8. The winners, the near misses and the individual dealership position are highlighted; so if you are not in the top tiers your position is treated confidentially.

Figure 4.7: Peugeot customer assessment

PEUGEOT CUSTOMER ASSESSMENT

Peugeot Experience – Purchase (Sales)

					Rank in Guild League
New Vehicle Buyer Questionnaire	XX	XX	XX	XX	XX
Sales Mystery Shopping – Physical	XX	XX	XX	XX	XX
Sales Mystery Shopping – Telephone	XX	XX	XX	XX	XX
Sub Total	XX	XX	XX	XX	XX

Peugeot Experience – Ownership (Aftersales)

Cust. Sat. Questionnaire – 12 mths	XX	XX	XX	XX	XX
Cust. Sat. Questionnaire – 24 mths	XX	XX	XX	XX	XX
Customer Contact Index	XX	XX	XX	XX	XX
Complaint Response Time	XX	XX	XX	XX	XX
Service Mystery Shopping – Telephone	XX	XX	XX	XX	XX
Sub Total	XX	XX	XX	XX	XX
TOTAL PEUGEOT CUSTOMER EXPERIENCE	XX	XX	XX	XX	XX
GRAND TOTAL	XX	XX	XX	XX	XX

Figure 4.8: The Guild of Gold Lion Dealers

LION STANDARDS

THE GUILD OF GOLD LION DEALERS

LEAGUE 1

Top 13 Qualify for Guild of Gold

1	xx
2	xxx
3	xxx
4	xx
5	xxxx
6	xx
7	xxxxx
8	xxx
9	xxx
10	xx
11	xxxxx
12	xxxx
13	xx

14	xxx
15	xx
16	xxxx
17	xxx
18	xx
19	xxxxx
20	xxx

Your League Position

26	xxxxx

4.4 *Support for dealerships*

A wide range of support services for dealers is provided which includes regular visits from Peugeot regional staff, weekly telephone contact with regional staff and six-monthly dealer conferences. The main voice of the dealer body is through the dealer council, an elected body of eight dealer representatives. This meets regularly –

as both a national council and a regional council – and on an *ad hoc* basis, when required, with senior Peugeot personnel. The objective of these meetings is to discuss policy, views and ideas and come to some mutual agreement recognising that 'you can never please everyone all of the time'. Peugeot commitment to these forums is demonstrated by the seniority of staff who attend; from the dealers' viewpoint this is a positive signal; it is the great strength of the system because 'everyone is busy enough, we do not want to waste time'.

Peugeot has been running an annual three-day conference for dealer accountants for the last ten years. The programme for 1995 consisted of a number of short keynote addresses, workshops, a business simulation game and a half-day leisure activity. This latter is particularly important. As one Peugeot manager commented:

> *the afternoon leisure activity ... is the only reward programme in the true sense for dealer accountants. This company, like most other organisations is very good at rewarding the sales people, the dealer principals ...*

For many delegates the most important part of the conference is to sit with other delegates for a reasonable length of time debating issues. In fact, this body suggested that the exchange of ideas was so valuable that more opportunities should be created. This led to the setting up of 'profit clinic groups' which started meeting four years ago. The group size is around twelve to fifteen geographically dispersed dealers. The programme consists of an informal dinner on day one followed by a full-day business meeting, where the dealers 'guardedly' share their individual dealership reports and interrogate one another.

4.5 *Discussion*

The strategy of the company in terms of market share and the provision of customer service is well understood throughout the organisation and is re-enforced by the sales plans and Lion Standards programme. However, there is a tension between trying to build a long-term relationship with the customer, developing loyalty to the marque, and the ever increasing service intervals which break the regular contact. One dealer summarised the problems:

> *we have all got to decide what we are going to do about that (the service intervals increasing on cars) it's the big question mark hanging over us all at the moment. Petrol vehicles have gone from six to nine thousand miles which creates problems in as much as the private owner tends now not to come in for a service ... it's creating all sorts of problems ... and of course we are asked to build this relationship with our customers ... for example, we do collection and delivery, that is very popular; we collect people's cars, service them, wash them and then take them back. With the service periods getting longer what's happening is the customer is not coming to the dealership anymore; some of them probably do not even know where we are ... With a fleet driver the difference between six and nine thousand miles may only be a fortnight, with the private owner it's a problem!*

Although the quality of the product has improved considerably there are still some problems with new cars. Most of these are intermittent, irritating problems which are very difficult to diagnose and are extremely annoying for both the customer and the service department. The frustration was summed up by one dealer:

> *I've got a master technician who has got equipment coming out of his ears, who has training coming out of his ears .... I think in certain areas the technology of the vehicle is in advance of the technology of diagnosis.*

Both the composite and the Lion Standards programme use internal benchmarking in terms of providing group average figures and top quartile figures for comparison. League tables are used for both the annual sales plan, compiled on a regional basis, and the Guild of Gold Lion Dealers, grouped according to sales volume. There are no league tables on financially-oriented measures, such as sales per employee, although dealers may choose to share this information at 'profit clinic' meetings; this is understandable given the ownership structure of the dealer network. While many dealers find the information provided invaluable in running their businesses there is an attitude among some dealers that 'their market place is unique' and 'their type of customer is different form the normal type of customer'; so comparisons with other dealerships are not relevant to them.

The incentives in terms of monetary rewards to the dealership are significant. There are tactical bonuses available for certain promotions but, for most dealers, it is the Lion Standards programme bonuses which make a significant contribution to profits. The documentation supporting the programme is clear and unambiguous.

An interesting feature in the scheme is the use of customer satisfaction questionnaires to assess the Peugeot Experience of after-sales customer service, 12 months and 24 months after purchase; this is entirely consistent with trying to develop a long-term relationship with the customer. In similar fashion, there is an interdependence between the dealers and Peugeot, described variously as a 'marriage' or 'partnership'. There are, inevitably, points of conflict, but the dealer council is an important channel of communication. As the following dealer commented:

> *there is a feeling that you have a direct line ... that your point of view has been listened to by someone who can take some action on it ... that's the strength of the dealer council system.*

4.6 Conclusions

Essentially, Peugeot is providing a range of cars and replacement parts for dealerships to sell to customers under strict conditions relating to the standards of service offered to those customers. Most of the dealerships are privately owned (Peugeot own 5 per cent of the dealership outlets which trade under the name Robins and Day, they trade under the same conditions as the rest of the dealerships), which obviously influences the nature and confidentiality of the information used to measure and improve performance.

The dominant features of the performance measurement systems described are the search for continuous improvement in aligning what is measured to strategic goals, and the ongoing review of the content and presentation of reports in line with user needs. In particular, the Lion Standards and composite are established programmes which have been developed and refined over their ten-year-plus life. In the Lion Standards programme the focus of reporting has changed from facilities to customer assessment of service quality. For the composite, the test was persuading the dealerships to contribute fairly detailed information on their financial performance, dealers will only provide that information if they perceive the report they receive as being useful to them. The fact that 85 per cent of franchises have joined the system is testament to this perceived usefulness. There is a belief that 'no one statistic will ever tell you the whole story ... you are trying to build up a picture'.

Inevitably, though, there are some areas of dissatisfaction with the measurement system. For example, there is some disquiet about the use of customer questionnaires. One dealer cited an internal questionnaire used in the service department of his dealership where one of the questions related to whether the customer considered he had received value for money. In this instance the 'no' box had been ticked; however, there was also a comment 'car repairs are never value for money'. The dealer was questioning the validity of using answers in isolation of the context.

The business is complicated, there are many facets to be considered and an acknowledgement by a senior Peugeot manager that:

> *when you introduce something ... no matter how successful you believe the programme is, actually being able to attach an improvement in a dealer's performance to the fact that he actually did anything in this programme is impossible. There are some areas where you can actually say 'wait a minute, you did that, and your customer questionnaire has proved that because you are now doing that, their previous dissatisfaction with the way you handled things has improved'. In global terms you cannot say to a dealer your workshop was slightly more efficient so you made £y extra profit this year compared to last year.*

This quote sums up the drive for continuous improvement, continuous review and the need for continuous communication between the dealers and Peugeot. The business is highly competitive, and European block exemption rules may force significant changes to the way dealership business is conducted. One dealer summed up his survival technique for adapting to changes in the car sales and servicing market:

> *I've got the essential things – commonsense and a sense of humour.*

5
Eversheds

I don't want a lawyer to tell me what I cannot do; I hire him to tell me how to do what I want to do.

J. Pierpont Morgan

5.1 Introduction

Eversheds is one of the country's largest commercial law practices with offices in London and eleven other commercial centres across England and Wales, and with over 200 partners and 700 fee earners (solicitors below partner level). The partnership was created from six leading firms from around the country which merged to provide a national legal service. Its clients consist of major UK and international public corporations, local and public authorities, and private businesses of all sizes. In particular, there is a strong concentration of manufacturing industry throughout its client base. The national firm consistently appears in the league tables of the top ten solicitors compiled by the *Hambro Company Guide* (Pritchard, *The Legal 500*, page 82). The office that is the subject of this chapter is the arm of Eversheds operating in one large region of the UK, where it is one of the leading law firms with around 35 partners and 150 other fee earners.

The firm's work is split into three main departments; company and commercial, litigation and property, though there are other smaller pockets of expertise in areas such as debt recovery and insolvency. Each department is headed by a team of partners and a number of fee earners and other support staff. The company and commercial department works for listed, USM and private companies advising on the legal implications of almost any aspect of corporate life, ranging from acquisitions, mergers, disposals and management buy-outs to consumer credit and finance house documentation and the exploitation of patents, trade marks, copyright and other intellectual property. Eversheds' clients tend to come to the litigation department with one of two objectives in mind: for advice on avoiding disputes or help in resolving those disputes that cannot be avoided. Again, the nature of the dispute might range from commercial fraud to employer discrimination and personal injury insurance claims. Third, the property department advises on any property transactions whether an individual's house purchase or (more usually) planned property developments of large plcs, such as the siting and building of a new factory, warehouse or superstore.

Whichever department forms the focus of activity for a particular client, the firm's publicity brochure sets out Eversheds' aim to offer existing and prospective clients 'the personal service, convenience and cost effectiveness of a leading [regional] practice, with the expertise and resources of a major national firm'. Thus Eversheds differentiates itself on the basis of:

(i) its credentials, *and*
(ii) the style and quality of service offered.

The firm's credentials are based on its established local presence – this particular arm of Eversheds has been at the heart of the local city business community for most of this century – and also its national network.

In terms of the style and quality of service offered, Eversheds sees itself as being friendly and accessible with an approach variously described in the brochure as 'energetic', 'sleeves-up' and founded on principles of 'commonsense'. In addition, it strives to keep the client informed of developments on a frequent and regular basis, and always to be available when needed. While charge-out rates are broadly similar to those of its direct competitors, Eversheds acknowledge that it is not the cheapest firm of lawyers. The emphasis then is 'adding value' to clients. Over time, the proof of this has to be through results. As one partner summarised:

> *The emphasis is on the delivery of a quality service. What clients want is absolute Rolls-Royce top-notch service at an affordable low price.*

Note that for Eversheds, as for its direct competitors (other large firms with a local presence), technical expertise is almost an axiomatic assumption; that is, the ability to actually do the job is an 'order-qualifying criteria'.

Although its credentials are important in attracting new clients, apart from the obvious need for solicitors to keep themselves updated technically, these credentials are not aspects of the business that are continuously under scrutiny. Instead, they remain fixed witnesses to the firm's structure and history. Thus, what is critical to the ongoing success of the partnership is the offering of a high quality of service, in terms of managing the legal task, cultivating and managing the relationship with the client, and in giving good value for money. The financial strength of Eversheds in terms of profitability, growth and positive cash flow is dependent on providing this level of service excellence.

5.2 The performance measurement system

Over the course of a year, Eversheds will carry out many thousand separate assignments or cases, varying from the very small lasting a matter of hours to the very large stretching over two or three years. Each individual fee earner will work on many different cases, several of which will be open at any one time. In describing the performance measurement system, then, a distinction will be made between measuring the performance of:

(a) a specific case; *and*
(b) an individual fee earner.

(a) Case performance

Figure 5.1 presents a map of the service process for a 'typical' assignment. Seven key aspects are identified from the initial approach from the client through to the client care visit following completion of the job. Clearly, all cases are different, particularly with respect to the time scales involved (this in itself has further implications for control within the partnership in terms of managing the product mix); none the less the model of service process is reasonably representative. For each of the seven 'events', an outline is given of the process, the monitoring system and performance measure(s) used.

1. Initial approach

The first event is concerned with gaining the business in the first place. Across each department there is a certain amount of core business producing a steady flow of work over a long period of time.

Figure 5.1: Eversheds – the service delivery process

Event	Service process	Monitoring system	Performance measures
1. Initial approach	Telephone call, referrals, repeat business	Target clients	–
2. Terms of engagement	Discussion with client regarding job and fees, etc.	Case file, letter of engagement	–
3. Legal investigation	Managing the job, managing the client	Case file, time sheets, 'green' sheets	Work-in-progress, problems (by exception)
4. Legal outcome	Transaction is completed, settlement is reached	Case file, 'green' sheets	Client satisfaction, problems (by exception)
5. Invoice raised	Chargeable hours and fees computed and processed	'Green' sheets, management accounts	Fee earner hours, fee earner fees
6. Cash received	Payment procedures	Aged debt by fee earner	Bad debts (by exception)
7. After-sales service	Client care visits	Target clients	Client satisfaction

There is also a proportion of work that arrives unsolicited, generally following telephone or written enquiries, or specific recommendation from existing clients. In addition, there are a number of potential clients, who may or may not have used Eversheds in the past, who are targeted by the firm through a variety of means including different types of corporate hospitality. This latter is also extended to existing clients in order to strengthen interrelationships and discover new opportunities. While the direct cost and time of such entertaining is easily quantifiable, little attempt is made to measure its effectiveness. As one of the financial administrators pointed out:

> *Now their [the partners'] argument would be that it is to generate future work – corporate hospitality – but my argument would be you should set a monthly figure for entertaining and then you should split it around the departments and the departments have to stick to that figure. If they are going to go over that figure, it needs to be discussed with the management part of that department who in turn could put the vote to the management committee. That is a very formal way of doing it, but those are the type of controls that I think we need to implement … like if you spend £X,000 on entertaining clients out in a year, you have got to say generate £Y,000 worth of fees to actually cover that.*

The current policy is not deliberate, but merely reflects the pattern of what has (not) been done on the past. In the short-term future it is likely that formal controls in this area will be introduced so that the effectiveness of this expenditure may be properly assessed.

2. Terms of engagement

At event 2, the precise job specification should be established as far as possible, given the often uncertain nature of investigating legal disputes. This will include the agreement of the fee charging mechanism, and the normal collection terms. In theory, a formal letter of engagement would be written up for each new assignment. However, for existing (large) clients this may be waived. As one company and commercial fee earner explained:

> *For a one-off client, if you've never heard of them before … then you negotiate your terms of engagement. But if it's somebody like XXXX, for whom we do a lot of work, they [the partner in charge] just say 'fine, get on with it'. You might mention it, but it looks silly if it is somebody you speak to every three weeks, saying it's £X per hour.*

3. *Legal investigation*

Event 3 is concerned with managing the job and the client; that is, actually carrying out the legal investigation. Here, whatever the nature of the case, the essential objective is to carry this out accurately, efficiently and effectively. One litigation partner described this need in some detail:

> *You've got to get your investigation of liability right to start with. Let's take a road traffic accident: you've got to make sure that you see the witnesses and go to the scene, or somebody goes to the scene, and takes photographs and draws plans. Getting the evidence right as to the happening of the accident is absolutely essential. There's nothing worse than ploughing along thinking you're OK and arriving in court with a witness saying something entirely different to what you expected. So you cannot risk that, especially with costs being what they are. You have to make sure that someone sees the witness right at the beginning, takes statements and assesses how they will do if it gets to court ... because somebody might look tremendous on paper but he might say anything when he's in the witness box. So that's the most important thing, and secondly, you're talking about personal injuries so you need to make sure that you get the right quality of medical evidence. We have expert medical witnesses that we can use up and down the country – neurologists, psychologists, psychiatrists etc. You will use the right medic to produce the right report.*

While each fee earner is expected to have, or be able to develop, the necessary technical expertise, a partner is always assigned to each case, and has a responsibility to review and discuss the progress on that case with the fee earner. This process is facilitated by the requirement to keep an up-to-date case file that includes *all* relevant information. One such piece of information is the amount of time spent working on the case. All staff submit daily time sheets, as shown in Figure 5.2, which break down their time into six-minute blocks, each of which is coded according to the client name and matter and the specific type of activity, for example, advocacy in court, attending a meeting or dictating a letter. Following the processing of time forms, the monthly 'green' sheets are produced. These are reports by the fee earners that summarise the current position on all their open files – the time spent on the case so far, how much work in progress there is, details of any interim bills invoiced, and whether these have been paid or not.

Figure 3.2 Eversheds time sheet for fee earners

F/E	Code	Name		No.	Date	Type

Line	Account Reference	Client Name and Matter	Time	Activity	Rate	Charge	Narrative
1							
2							
3							
4							
5							
6							
7							
8							
9							
10							
11							
12							
13							
14							
15							
			Total Time			Total Charge	

A ADVOCACY
C ATTENDANCE (CLIENT)
D OTHER DICTATION
J IN COURT
J TRAVELLING

L LETTER DICTATION
M MEETING (OTHERS)
P PREPARATION
T TELEPHONE
W WAITING

X UNSPECIFIED
90 HOLIDAYS
91 SICKNESS
92 PUBLIC RELATIONS

93 OFFICE ADMINISTRATION
94 CLIENT NON-CHARGEABLE
95 MISCELLANEOUS
96 EVERSHEDS
97 FURTHER EDUCATION

98 SEMINARS
99 ARTICLED CLKS/WRITING ARTS

Where these green sheets highlight a specific problem, this would be discussed in the first instance between the fee earner in charge of the case and the partner assigned to it, and subsequently, if necessary, at the management committee meeting.

4. Legal outcome

Event 4 represents the completion of the legal side of the case. Appraising performance in this area, however, is more difficult. For some assignments, success might be measured in terms of whether the transaction went through; for others, though, success is a less straightforward concept to define. A senior solicitor within the litigation department seemed quite philosophical about this:

> *In a sense you can never get a good result. Litigation is to some extent a thankless job because your client really only wants to get back what he thinks he's always been entitled to, and resents having to pay for it. His time and the time of his managers isn't recoverable generally in litigation, and it tends to be a wretched nuisance. They come when they have a problem, and they come to lawyers usually when they have done all they can do in-house.*

In all cases any concrete evidence of client satisfaction is welcomed, perhaps a small token of appreciation or simply a letter of thanks. However, these are relatively rare and often the most obvious sign of client satisfaction is on the occurrence of repeat business. On the relatively infrequent occasions where clients are *dissatisfied*, they are more forward in making their feelings known.

5. Invoice raised

Following the completion of the legal investigation an invoice is prepared by the fee earner, approved by the partner and dispatched to the client. Clearly, the amounts charged would be in accordance with the terms agreed in event 2, either formally or informally.

6. Cash received

Normal credit terms of one month generally apply, but there is an understandable reluctance to chase overdue debts, especially those relating to the larger clients. To some extent there remains a feeling among the fee earners that troubling clients for money with whom they establish close working relationships isn't really 'the decent thing to do'. The financial administrator pointed out that:

> *Responsibility stops at the partners. What basically happens with credit control is we have various stages. We do our clients a monthly statement; when the invoice comes to X days old we issue a demand letter to them and of course you get to the stage where you cannot send a demand letter to him as he is a good client. My argument back is, well, he is not a good client because he does not pay his bill.*

7. After-sales service

The seventh and final stage of the service delivery process is the client care visit, which should be carried out, usually by a partner, with all major clients. This has a two-fold purpose as described by one partner in the property department:

> *You are actually asking them to sit down for ten minutes, an hour, whatever you think is appropriate and we will look back on the previous year at the things we have done, say whether the job was good, bad or indifferent and also, and this is extremely important, you spend a bit of time looking forward ... what is coming up in the coming year? What are your plans? ... How can we help?*

(b) Fee earner performance

Essentially three performance measures are seen as critical in the appraisal of individual fee earners. The first two relate directly to the volume of work undertaken by that fee earner; specifically the number of *chargeable hours* worked, and the amount of *chargeable fees* earned. The third criterion is '*mistakes*' made.

For almost all fee earners there is a standard chargeable hours target set for partners and a slightly higher one for all others. The distinction reflects the substantial amount of client-centred but non-chargeable work that partners are involved with, as well as their managerial responsibilities within the firm. Actual performance against these targets is updated and monitored monthly on the basis of time sheet submissions. A subsidiary measure currently being developed by the financial controller is the ratio of chargeable time to total time:

> *the more we can tweak the chargeable bit the more fees we can get coming in. As a rule of thumb consultants tend to work on the principle that if they can get 60 per cent of their time chargeable then they're OK.*

In theory the amount of chargeable fees earned by a fee earner should be his or her chargeable hours multiplied by their standard charge-out rate per hour. Sometimes in practice, though, there will be adjustments to these rates depending on the underlying circumstances. A specific target for fees earned by each fee earner is set at the beginning of the year to reflect an appropriate level of adjustments. Actual fees earned are extracted from billings each month, and monitored against target.

The third performance indicator, 'mistakes', is not actually measured formally, and while there is a widespread acknowledgement that the idea of one mistake and you're out is exaggerated, nevertheless it is well understood that:

> *You can do ten pieces of good work and it will be forgotten. You can do one piece of rubbishy work and people will remember five years later and it will come back to haunt you.*

A mistake could take many different forms from careless technical errors to falling short of quality of service standards such as:

> *Saying it is X when it should be Y. Not ringing people back, not writing to people when you said you would write to them, not ringing people back when they ring complaining about you not ringing them back.*

Occasional shortfalls of this kind are probably inevitable, though one purpose of the extensive training courses attended by fee earners on the one hand, and the partner presence on each case on the other, is to reduce the risk of such oversights. Echoing these controls, the senior partner commented that:

> *The one unforgivable mistake is not to seek advice.*

The green sheets and relatively new staff appraisal schemes are seen as important, but very much secondary to the three indicators above.

Eversheds do not incorporate any sophisticated performance-related bonus scheme to act as an incentive for partners and other fee earners to achieve their targets. For partners, the financial reward is their profit share at the year end. This is calculated by dividing overall partnership profits by the number of partners, all receiving an equal share. Thus, the size of the payoff is dependent on the performance of the partnership as a whole, not solely on the partner's performance of their own sphere of influence. As emphasised by one property partner, this distribution method reinforces the teamwork ethic within the firm, and avoids departmental empire building:

> *If you started rewarding partners by reference to the performance of their teams or departments, then what would happen is ... you would build up your own olympo wouldn't you? If my earnings depended on my individual billing I would recruit a property litigator and a corporate lawyer because a lot of my clients would produce that work. At the moment I wander along the corridor and give it to the litigation department or along to see someone in the company department and say here is a corporate requisition or here is a piece of commercial work for my client. Look after him and give him back to me when you have finished with him. There would be a massive disincentive to doing that if we were not all one team.*

For other fee earners, the incentive to perform is equally transparent; the prospect of becoming a partner of the firm when sufficient experience has been gained.

5.3 *Commentary*

Eversheds differentiates itself on the basis of its credentials and its high quality of service. Technical excellence is assumed. In helping to drive this strategy forward throughout the business the role of the performance measurement system is rather subtle. It is implicated, but only indirectly. Instead there are three key ingredients to the operationalisation of the firm's strategy – the professionalism of the fee earners, the career structure for the fee earners, and the organisational structure and office atmosphere.

5.3.1 *Professionalism*

The key performance indicators already discussed – chargeable hours, chargeable fees, and no mistakes – are clear, unambiguous quantifiable measures. However, they do not directly reflect quality. The accepted wisdom is that only by offering the required quality of service will fee earners be able to meet their targets, since consistently poor-quality work would not lead to partners delegating further work. Thus, the bottom line is justified as a catch-all fee earner performance measure, despite it representing the results of success rather than the determinants of it. As one partner reinforced:

> *The shock that you get on becoming a fee earner and even more a*
> *partner is suddenly there is an environment where there are no marks*
> *out of ten, there is no degree at the end of it, there is nothing like that at*
> *all. … That is the greatest shock, how do you test yourself? In a sense*
> *your fees show you are working.*

So, how else do fee earners measure the quality of what they are
doing? This varies from individual to individual, but each is likely to
develop certain habits that govern how they handle their cases. For
example, the following two extracts describe examples of self-
regulatory measures used by a partner and a senior solicitor
respectively:

> *I will never sell anything I do not understand. If I am doing a*
> *presentation I will prepare for it. You can then argue you're not being*
> *cost effective, well I accept that, but if I am going to do presentations I*
> *make sure I know what I am talking about. If you make sure your team*
> *do likewise you increase your hit rate.*

> *I always say even if you just ring your client to say nothing is happening*
> *that's a very positive thing. I mean I fail to a certain degree if my clients*
> *have to ring me to say 'look, what's happening?' because I think I*
> *should be ringing them … at the end of the week … or on some [other]*
> *regular basis.*

Thus, the quality of work done relies on this notion of the
professionalism of the staff involved, with its consequent implications
for honesty, integrity, reliability, accuracy, thoroughness and attention
to detail. None of these is formally measured. A further, though again
unmeasured, characteristic is the requirement for fee earners to be
flexible in their client dealings, to discern how their performance
needs to be modified to meet the demands of specific individuals.
For example, one partner mentioned:

> *I have one client who insists on consulting me about everything and even*
> *then if I bring in a specialist from another department, he will speak to*
> *me to check that advice even though I am not as qualified. That is what*
> *he is comfortable with, so that is what I have to deliver. You cannot*
> *have a set of rules that says we will always do it like this for every client,*
> *it has to be client driven. You have to be all things to all men in the sense*
> *of the style and also the tactics you adopt to please the client – it has to be*
> *the style and the tactics that they want, rather than what we say they*
> *want.*

Similarly, the nature of what the client care visit comprises may vary: some clients ... require a very formal approach to it. We will send them a questionnaire and they will sit for two hours and go over it and answer it, and they will dictate a ten-page letter in reply analysing every nuance. For others it is a pint in the pub; it just depends on the nature of the client and what you think they are comfortable with.

Again, it is the bottom line that remains the measured focus of attention; that is the impact of professionalism, quality and flexibility on chargeable hours and fees.

5.3.2 *Career structure for fee earners*

For qualified solicitors and senior solicitors the big carrot is the possibility of becoming a partner within the firm. Currently, there is no written specification of the characteristics required for a partner, although there is a feeling that it is becoming increasingly difficult to make the transition. This reflects the constraint on growth enforced by the economic climate, and also the existing partners' age profile. The Eversheds' office studied for this report is a young firm with many partners in their thirties or early forties. Few retire young, so there is not a regular cycle of partnership vacancies. Consequently, one existing partner suggested that:

Increasingly the appointment of partners will have to be justified on hard business grounds. It is probably fair to say that in the past there has been what I call the 'good chap test' ... I think the time has come where we have actually got to set out in writing what we think the criteria are for people to apply for a partner so they know what it is they have got to achieve.

So what do they have to achieve? Among staff interviewed there was a high degree of consensus concerning the characteristics of a 'good' solicitor, including: 'a good grounding in and thorough understanding of the law'; 'practical and procedural knowledge'; 'commercial nous'; 'good communication skills'; 'motivation and commitment'; 'honesty and integrity'; 'speed and accuracy'; 'personality'; 'an ability to cultivate relationships'; 'professional understanding, no bull'. While in terms of the characteristics necessary for promotion to partner, the following fee earner's extract illustrates that although they are hard to define, people are implicitly aware of them.

> *I think that may be a perception again to bring in a lot of fees, but I don't think it's just about producing vast amounts of money; I think there are other elements. There probably is an element of being recognised as being the best at what you do, or particularly good at what you do. ... What's interesting if you follow it through is how unsurprised people are when the new partners are announced – it is clearly something that says they're going to be a partner.*

There is also a commonly held view that in view of the scarcity of partnership vacancies it is unlikely that simply meeting chargeable hours and fee targets would be sufficient. It is considered that the real high fliers would be achieving well in excess of this, perhaps as many as 300 extra chargeable hours during the year. This demonstrates the cost of success in terms of workload. Given the estimated 60 per cent chargeable proportion of time the normal target workload implies something approaching a 50-hour working week (allowing for five weeks annual holiday). To achieve 'high-flier' hours and still have some holiday would imply an average working week of around 60 hours, unless non-chargeable time could be significantly reduced. However, this might be potentially damaging if cuts were made in the amounts of research and training. Nor is the situation alleviated once promotion has been awarded. As one partner commented:

> *My wife thinks working one day at weekends is the norm, it is a six-day week basically.*

Nevertheless, it is still the goal of partnership that drives the fee earners to achieve the target hours and fees set for them, and therefore to conform to the high standards of quality required by the firm. As such, competitive pressures that impact on the volume of work in the future may lead to motivational difficulties for fee earners only too aware of the increasingly narrow opportunities for advancement within Eversheds.

5.3.3 *Organisational structure and office atmosphere*

As noted earlier, the organisation is split into three main departments – company and commercial, litigation and property – while within these departments fee earners may be divided into separate work teams. Although this formal structure might in theory give rise to a set of small independent practices that have little contact with one another, in practice Eversheds has retained a broader teamwork ethic where most people know each other, first name terms are generally used, and most partners adopt an open door policy. This friendly, informal atmosphere is immediately apparent when visiting the office, and many staff feel this is an important consideration in attracting clients as it gives the impression of people who are warm and genuine, as opposed to the more traditional image of lawyers as being rather distant and aloof. This, of course, is also an attractive aspect of the firm to fee earners themselves. As one commented:

> *I think it's much easier to come into a place where it's warm and friendly and the secretaries have a laugh and you can stand within the secretarial bay and join in with that, than it is to go into a firm where everybody has got their head down and the door is shut.*

However, in the future there are two pressures which might threaten this friendly atmosphere. First, the economic environment and competitive forces may reduce the amount of funds available for spending within the organisation, in which case the level of investment in the staff infrastructure might easily be an early casualty. The financial administrator offered the following warning:

> *We spend a fair amount of money on the staff dinner dance every year. We go to the Majestic at XXXX and the firm lays on buses to take the staff there and bring them back. You take your wife, husband, boyfriend or girlfriend … there is a bottle of wine per person on the table and there is a free bar when you first go in, and entertainment. That costs a lot of money. Then also the firm gives each member of staff £10 to go out departmentally at Christmas, and we have a departmental Christmas dinner as well. I think those are the kind of things that could be in danger; it depends on how financially aware the partners become.*

If these kinds of event were to disappear, there would be an adverse impact on morale, there being no chance to 'let your hair down together' as reward for all the hours worked. Also, it would reduce the opportunities to meet colleagues from different departments and so, over time, lead to a more disjointed organisation. While the consequence of the second threat is similar, its source, conversely, is the continued success of the organisation. If growth rates are sustained in the future with further vacancies at partner and fee earner level, then again the carefully cultivated office atmosphere might begin to suffer with visiting clients perceiving a large, formal, multi-layered organisation rather than a friendly, down-to-earth set of people who are there to help. However, not all staff interviewed agreed with this view. For example, one partner suggested:

> *I do not think it [growth] really matters ... provided you organise*
> *yourselves through the team meetings, weekends away or whatever. ... I*
> *know all the fee earners in our department on first name terms but in other*
> *departments, no. Already, there are so many now as the firm has grown*
> *that you cannot keep up if you do not work with them. I do not think it is*
> *the partner to fee earner [relationship] you have to watch, I think it is the*
> *partner to partner as you get bigger even within departments.*

5.4 Conclusions and the future

While it is important to retain a balance in a performance
measurement system between formal and informal measures, and
between standardised and prescriptive measures, there are some
notable gaps in the framework at Eversheds. Stages 1 to 4 of the
service delivery process are not really formally assessed at all,
monitoring mostly being left to the discretion of the team leader on a
monthly basis, although even this process would seem to be variable.
It is not apparent, for example, that there are standardised procedures
for producing letters of engagement, and for monitoring them from
time to time for quality, accuracy, completeness and timeliness.
Instead, the quality of service provided on a specific job is often
assumed to be high, and seems to be left to the professionalism of the
staff involved. As such, the formal performance measurement system
focuses predominantly on the staff rather than on individual cases.

The key question is whether this system of performance measures
captures the essence of Eversheds' overall objectives of profitability,
growth and offering a high-quality service. Broadly, the answer to this
is *yes*, but with the proviso that it is because Eversheds *is* profitable that
little need is perceived for any more involved systems of performance
measurement and control. If this profitability was threatened then
actions might be taken at the margin as a result of the lack of more
formalised monitoring systems – and the implications of such actions
would be unclear. Clearly, the most obvious such threat is the
combination of the general recession in the economy and the actions of
competitors in closing the quality gap. Several consequences of, and
possible responses to, this threat have already been explored within
this chapter. However, as there is increased pressure on the level of
fees earned, one deliberate response of the partnership has been to
'pass the learning down', with junior staff taking on more
responsibility. This has led, for instance, to a noticeable difference in
the work profile of the secretaries. As one observed:

You used to be just a typist but nowadays they realise they get more for their money if a secretary does make phone calls, and that she can be trusted with doing meetings. ... I've seen it since working for X for the last three years, I've seen it because he just gives me everything. Because it's a waste of his time; I might as well do it. He's charging a lot of money while he's sat there during all these meetings and I have noticed that more and more fee earners are being encouraged to let their secretaries fill out forms and things whereas bosses used to do that.

It should be stressed that this process has been handled very carefully, with individual members of staff both keen and ready to be given more challenging work. There are, however, two potential issues associated with this move towards more delegation. First, as this response is incremental, that is, on a case by case basis, adverse implications may not become apparent. Over a period of time, the danger is that the quality of service suffers, as the ability of staff to undertake their assignments may become compromised. Second, many clients like to deal with a partner. In the following extract, one existing partner half-jokingly expounded an answer to this dilemma.

Well, I think the market will be increasingly competitive. I think the skill will be to ensure that the work is delegated to people who are not as expensive but do a good job. Clients are increasingly sophisticated. Look at the position of the Americans. They like to deal with partners, so the way the Americans have got round it is that they call what we call partners 'shareholders', and they call the associates who are qualified 'partners' and then all the others are called 'associates'. So they all have a big title.

It may not come to this. Nevertheless, as the business environment does continue to become more competitive, Eversheds' differentiation strategy, based essentially on a high quality of service, may need to be supported by a more well-defined performance measurement system. This system should more closely monitor determinants of success on a regular basis, rather than focusing exclusively on the outputs of that success, namely the amount of chargeable hours and fees thereby earned. This change would not only enable Eversheds to guard against any potential fall in standards, but also would allow the encouragement of an ethic of continuous improvement, and so reinforce their source of competitive advantage.

5.5 *Addendum*

The series of interviews with personnel at Eversheds took place between the months of May and July 1994. This chapter describes, therefore, an organisation at a particular point in its history. As would be expected within any dynamic business entity, internal structures and systems develop over time, and certainly Eversheds has moved forward significantly since the interview period.

First, as an organisation Eversheds has now been formally created as a national firm, with the regional titles being dropped, and with a large London firm added to cement the organisation's overall competitive position in the UK. Second, the Law Society's requirements for good practice have improved; in particular, the sending out of terms and conditions to clients and the reinforcement of this by way of a letter of engagement on almost every job as a client's right. Systems have arisen to monitor this. Third, the career structures within the firm have been more clearly defined, with more precise criteria set out to merit promotion to senior solicitor and partner. Fourth, a great deal of work is being done on the development and implementation of quality control procedures in general; one area, referred to earlier in the chapter, where this is already very apparent is in relation to monitoring the effectiveness of entertainment expenditure.

The sheer size of the business and the reality of the competitive environment have meant that the firm cannot simply carry on in the future adopting control procedures that were adequate in the past. The partners' good sense, professionalism and gut feeling remain necessary, but are no longer sufficient. The firm has clearly recognised this and taken steps to develop accordingly. Eversheds has not stood still.

Either next year or the year after, Arthur Andersen will probably overtake Coopers & Lybrand to become the UK's largest firm – a remarkable achievement for a firm that was not even in the UK 40 years ago.

Accountancy, July 1995

6.1 Background

The Arthur Andersen worldwide organisation is one of the largest accountancy and consulting firms in the world employing over 80,000 people worldwide with offices in over 75 countries. The partnership provides a comprehensive range of financial and businesses services to clients. It has a reputation for the breadth, depth and excellence of the financial services which it offers its many and varied clients. It provides audit and business advisory services, financial, taxation and business consultancy to businesses and individuals.

Andersens operates a 'one-firm concept' throughout the partnership, guaranteeing its quality of service across the world. One partner has overall responsibility for any one client, whatever the mix of services required by the client, and that partner has the authority to command resources worldwide, if necessary. Standard methods and planning procedures are used worldwide, with all staff being highly trained providing a uniform level of high quality in systems, processes and people. It has invested in a 'global best practice knowledge database' giving access to leading edge business practices from around the world to enhance client service. The partnership has seen constant growth, with profits shared on a worldwide basis.

In 1995, in the UK league table of the top 50 UK accounting firms, measured by fee income, Andersens reached second position behind Coopers & Lybrand and in front of KPMG, Ernst & Young, Price Waterhouse and Touche Ross. In the UK, Andersens operates through thirteen regional offices, and all offices provide a full range of services, although the mix of those services varies from regional office to regional office. All offices have access to central databases and there is great stress on knowledge-sharing to improve processes and customer service. Although staff are attached to a particular office there is some flexibility of movement between offices for specified periods, to cover temporary staff shortfalls or for particular jobs such as corporate recovery, where staff with specific areas of expertise may need to be brought together at fairly short notice.

This chapter focuses on the audit and business advisory, tax and corporate recovery services provided by a UK regional office.

6.2 Strategy

The partnership expresses its aim as being the premier accounting organisation both in the UK and internationally. Critical to the success of the partnership is offering a consistently high quality of service, in terms of managing the technical task, and managing the relationship with the client through providing consistent standards, culture, quality and approach throughout the worldwide organisation. The financial strength of Andersens, in terms of profitability and growth, is dependent on providing this high level of service and in 1995 its UK fee income was £539.5 million. For Andersens and its direct competitors the ability to undertake the technical job is an 'order-qualifying criterion' – it is a necessary condition. The 'order-winning criteria' which Andersens believes differentiate it in the market place are its reputation, the style and quality of service offered and its worldwide partnership network.

6.3 The service

Andersens offers a range of services to its clients from annual audit and tax planning to corporate recovery services. There is a danger in today's highly specialised financial world that professional advice could become fragmented; clients could find themselves constantly briefing different 'specialists' on the nature of their business. Andersens tackles this communication issue by giving one partner overall responsibility for any one client. That partner plans and co-ordinates all the services on behalf of his client and has authority to command resources worldwide, if necessary. The mix of services required by individual clients will vary depending on the size of the client's organisation, the nature of the business, the economic climate faced and their financial situation. In this sense every job is different, some lasting a few days to others lasting several months. This places significant demands on the performance monitoring and measurement systems used.

While all cases are different, particularly in terms of the amount of time spent and the spread of that time (for example, audit jobs have a fairly intensive period of activity at the year end whereas a tax planning job may be spread out over several months), there are common elements to every job. Figure 6.1 represents the service delivery process which comprises six key 'events', from initial contact through to cash being received (normally) following the completion of the job.

Events 3 to 6 are tightly monitored, both formally and informally, throughout the organisation. Event 1, getting the business, is more problematic. There is a dual aspect here; first in retaining established clients and second in recruiting new clients. Established clients have evidence of the previous quality of work and the task is to maintain the client/partner-responsible relationship. Potential clients are targeted at partner planning meetings and various presentations, social events, sponsorships, partner visits, etc., are arranged for both the potential and established clients. While the expenses of these initiatives are easily measured, their effectiveness, in terms of getting business, is not.

Event 2, defining the job, is viewed as a key area because every job is different, clients have different expectations and a 'happy client' pays up readily and will repeat business. Andersens devotes considerable energy at the outset in trying to define exactly what the client wants, the time scale involved and the budget. This is formally recorded in a letter of engagement which can be referred to during the contract period. The feasibility of producing a letter of engagement is partly a function of the service offered: for example, it is much more difficult to forecast the complexities and hence the time needed on a corporate recovery job compared with a routine audit.

Event 3 amounts to 'doing the job'. The team allocated to the job, through the job scheduling system, will reflect the nature and perceived complexity of the task. Progress is measured against budget; this gives early warning of potential problems such as whether the job is likely to overrun because the level of complexity

Figure 6.1: Arthur Andersen – the service delivery process

Event	Service process	Monitoring system	Performance measures
1. Initial approach	Telephone call, repeat business, external referrals, internal referrals	Partner review, target clients	Partner visits, presentations, entertainments, sponsorships
2. Terms of engagement	Discussion with client	Planning meetings	Letters of engagement
3. Audit/consultancy/tax/CRS investigations	Managing the job, managing the client	Job file, time sheets, managing partner visit to clients	Quality review by managing partner, work-in-progress, fee adjustments
4. Outcome	Report delivered	Rating forms, time sheets	Client satisfaction, staff review
5. Invoice issued	Time and expense sheets processed and agreed by job manager	Time sheets, management accounts	Fees charged
6. Cash received	Payment follow-up procedures	Aged debt	Debtor days

was underestimated or because of staff problems. For larger jobs a managing partner will be assigned. The role of this partner is to oversee the quality of the job by reviewing documentation and, equally importantly, discussing progress with the client. It is important that this reviewing process takes place during the job so that any problems or issues are identified and can be handled immediately.

All 'assistants' and 'seniors' are evaluated on a rating form after every job (event 4). The performance measurement and appraisal systems for staff are described in section 6.4.2. All professional staff complete time sheets. These form the basis of billing to the clients so it is important that they are accurate and up to date. Time allocations for audit work are in units of 30 minutes whereas tax work is recorded in six-minute units. This largely reflects the nature of the work where audit occurs in large blocks of time whereas tax tends to be more widely spread. A bill is prepared and has to be reviewed and agreed by the job manager before it is issued to the client. The responsibility for collecting the fee is passed to the credit controller (event 6). If problems arise with payment the office financial controller will be involved and a plan of action will be agreed with the job manager.

6.4 Facilitating the service

The service is highly labour intensive with a large proportion of staff having direct contact with clients. The performance measurement systems focus predominately on staff. This section describes the two performance measurement systems related to staff, one at the office level in terms of general practice management and the other at the individual level in terms of the staff rating and appraisal system.

6.4.1 General practice management

Office organisation

The office is headed by a managing partner and organised into four divisions three providing specialised professional services directly to the client in the areas of audit and business advice, tax and corporate recovery services. The fourth division is practice management and services, which provides personnel and recruitment services, financial control, administration and secretarial services.

The staff

For monitoring purposes staff are classified between 'support' and 'practice'. The distinguishing factor between the two classifications is that support staff (that is, all practice management staff which includes the financial controller, personnel and recruitment manager, computer support, secretarial and administration) do not have their time charged directly to clients while practice staff do. There are four levels of practice staff – partners, managers, seniors and assistants – with clearly defined roles within the organisation. These roles dictate the amount of time that should be charged to clients: for example, partners are expected to devote time to gaining new business, that is, practice development, so less of their time is charged directly to clients than, say, managers whose role is predominately delivering the service to clients.

Two sets of performance measures follow naturally from the staff classification:

- headcount;
- chargeable time.

Headcount

A key issue for control is 'managing the pyramid'. The pyramid refers to the ratios of partners to managers to seniors to assistants employed, see Figure 6.2. Andersens has a clear notion, developed over the years, of an ideal shape of the pyramid which will lead to profitability and growth of the business.

Figure 6.2: The staff pyramid

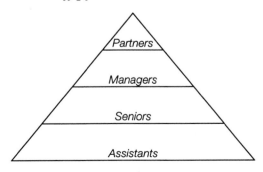

The shape of the pyramid is different for the three professional divisions for instance – audit has proportionately more assistants than tax and corporate recovery services – so the notion of an ideal shape of the pyramid is linked to the mix of business provided and varies from office to office. In addition, headcount reports measure the ratio of support staff to practice staff. This ratio is monitored monthly on a regional basis. This is an important control variable because it is akin to measuring overheads in the sense that support staff are not directly charged to clients. Individual offices are able to benchmark their performance in this area by reviewing the monthly regional summary reports which show the ratio of support staff to practice staff; this is keenly monitored by the office financial controller.

Chargeable time

Chargeable time is the amount of staff time which is directly charged to a client. Each staff layer in the pyramid has a target amount of chargeable time. As with the shape of the pyramid these chargeable time targets have been built up from experience within the organisation. There is an acknowledgement that although exceeding the targets may lead to increased short-term profitability, if this was at the expense of training, for example, it may lead to a drop in longer-term quality and hence profitability problems.

Training

Andersens prides itself on its extensive staff training programmes which are driven by the philosophy of providing a uniform level of quality throughout the world, all staff being trained to exacting standards. The significant costs are monitored regionally on a monthly basis (see Table 6.1).

Table 6.1: Training investment per person

Region	Total training costs, £	Total cumulative headcount	Average cumulative cost per person, £
	Audit and business advisory group	Audit and business advisory group	Audit and business advisory group
	Tax group	Tax group	Tax group
	Admin group	Admin group	Admin group
	Total region	*Total region*	*Total region*

6.4.2 *Staff rating and appraisal*

There is a clearly defined career structure for practice staff from
assistant to senior to manager to partner – the pyramid structure. Staff
who join the organisation are under no illusions as to the future. This
is 'an up or out organisation', 'you are better paid but have to work
harder', 'it's a meritocracy'. Practice staff tend to be recruited directly
from university, after completing an undergraduate degree, and are
appointed as assistants. There are no career seniors or partners, staff
either get promoted or leave, 'it's a pyramid structure'. Regular
counselling and performance appraisal is provided for everyone. The
process and regularity of staff evaluation varies with staff grade, and
to a lesser extent with division. Initially, some staff find this process
threatening but there is general consensus that it is used in a positive
manner and is appreciated for that.

Partners

Partners are reviewed every two years via the partner evaluation
system, and financial rewards are directly related to this review. The
first part of the process is a peer group review by division head,
managing partner and any other partner the reviewer may have
worked with. The results of this review are passed to a central
(worldwide) review committee and this committee takes a
comparative view on partner performance throughout the
organisation, so that equity between partners is maintained on a
worldwide basis. Each partner is awarded a number of 'units' which
determines their share of the worldwide earnings (allowances are
made for cost of living and exchange rate adjustments). It is possible
for the review committee to award a reduction in units. The 'unit'
earnings of all partners, worldwide, is published; however, the
distribution of this information is restricted to partners.

Managers

Every manager has a strictly confidential annual review with his
counselling partner. The process is driven by an annual reporting
document, sections of which are completed by the manager prior to
interview. The personnel department adds factual details such as
courses attended and planned and then the form is completed by the
counselling partner during the interview. The outcome of this process
is an agreed set of actions, by the individual manager and the firm, to
achieve objectives for future personal and career development.

Target dates for achieving the actions are agreed and responsibility for the firm's actions is assigned to a particular individual.

Seniors and assistants

Seniors and assistants are evaluated after every job by the manager or senior they have been working for. The document used to discuss performance is a rating form: 'it is the primary piece of documentation which provides evidence of an individual's performance – across the board performance'. The form contains detailed questions grouped in six areas:

- technical skills;
- quality of work product;
- job ownership and wrap-up;
- people development;
- client service;
- professional attributes.

An overall evaluation is provided at the end of the form with a ranking scale from 'exceptional performance' to 'performance is below what is expected of an individual at the level of experience both in the present job and the requirement to demonstrate long-term potential for progression within the firm', the latter rating being problematic for an individual. Extensive guidance notes are provided for the reviewer responsible for completing the form. The sources of information suggested for the reviewer are the quality of the work product, client's comments and observation of the individual in action. The review process is treated seriously, clear advice being given on conducting the review discussion which includes giving praise and thanks for work well done and providing constructive criticism, where appropriate. There is an emphasis on asking for, and listening to, individuals' views. The outcome is a rating for the individual plus a series of suggestions for improving performance.

Secretarial staff are evaluated every three months. The review ranges from technical competence to personal appearance and conduct. The outcome is a rating from 1 'far exceeds job requirements' to 5 'does not meet job requirements', plus identification of training needs which could improve skills.

The importance which Andersens attaches to staff appraisal is evidenced by the time devoted to the appraisal process, their frequency and the positive way in which they are used. This is captured in the declaration at the top of every appraisal form:

It is the firm's policy to develop the competence and creative ability of all its employees to their fullest potential.

The purpose of the performance appraisal and evaluation report is to provide a basis for:

- *Feedback on the quality of work, highlighting strengths and areas for improvement;*
- *Counselling and setting objectives to assist in the development of skills and abilities.*

6.5 Discussion

6.5.1 Arthur Andersen's strategy

The partnership expresses its aims as being the premier accounting organisation both regionally and internationally by providing a quality service which will lead to growth and profitability. The consistent message is that to fulfil this strategy the key issue driving the business is to gain, develop and cultivate 'happy clients'. This is facilitated by the technical expertise of staff and the degree and level of communication provided between staff and between staff and clients. Like many service organisations a high proportion of Andersens' staff have direct customer contact, from partners responsible for individual clients to assistants working for long periods at a client's premises on, for example, an audit assignment. These issues have implications for the type of staff Andersens recruits, the degree of training given and the focus of the performance measurement system on the staff review process.

6.5.2 Routes to service quality

The one worldwide firm concept is encouraged by all staff being trained to exacting technical standards throughout the organisation. Many courses are run on an international basis so employees have the opportunity to meet and study with colleagues from around the world. This in turn provides consistent standards throughout offices and consequently facilitates both project and staff sharing.

Knowledge is shared through national and international technical meetings and access to Andersens' worldwide databases such as the global best practices database. In terms of technical service staff comments include the conviction that 'our audit practice is two to three years ahead of our competitors', 'we give a superior tax service ... we are more imaginative, more creative', 'we are seen to be at the cutting edge of tax ... our tax software is by far and away the best quality tax software on the market'.

Considerable emphasis is placed on the importance of managing the client relationship from the initial setting-up of a project, and managing its process and progress to project completion. Experience has shown that communication with the client is crucial. This is achieved in three specific ways: by establishing exactly what the client wants, keeping the client informed during the process and measuring client satisfaction at the end of the project. Three quotes from Andersen staff demonstrate these points:

> *We try to establish up front as openly as possible, based on discussions with our client first of all, what do you want from this engagement, and if it is audit, clearly what they want is an unqualified audit report. In addition they want the audit process to go quickly, they want it to be non-disruptive, they want to pay as little as possible and they want the same bloke as they had last year.*

> *For example, if you are doing a flotation which typically won't go entirely according to plan – something mucks it up. When that happens one of two things can happen; you either go into a bolt hole and you are in a complete flurry with your people or you come out of it, you do a great job and at the end of the job you made the deadline. Unfortunately, the client has not seen this so when you go and tell the client that 'actually in order to do this we had to spend twice as much time on it, now let's talk about the bill' the client will turn round and say 'I am not very happy about this'. The other approach is when the problem happens you are close enough to your client to say, immediately, 'alright, this has happened, what shall we do about this.' You take the client along with you. You share the problem with the client and you agree with the client what you need to do to get round the problem. ... That transparency is very important.*

> *I think the most important thing is a 'happy client' and a client is not one person, it is a whole collection of people including subsidiary people, finance people ... there are increasingly a larger number of stakeholders*

> *interested in how we perform with a client. The key performance measure is client satisfaction and we instituted ...... a rather more formal programme of ascertaining clients' satisfaction over the last two to three years and certainly most of our larger clients are asked on a reasonably formal basis ... about our responsiveness, our people, whether they have seen enough of the right people, what they think of our people and that is typically done by the managing partner.*

The driving force behind the first two quotes is 'no surprises'. Terms and conditions for the project are set out and agreed up front and any problems encountered during the project are shared and discussed with the client during the process. The final comment demonstrates the commitment to client satisfaction. Andersens has demonstrated through client research in the USA ('we are constantly measuring everything in the States') that higher levels of satisfaction with its services leads to significantly better fee recoveries thus affecting bottom line earnings of the organisation. This is obviously important in a fiercely competitive environment and this research led to a worldwide push to formalise client satisfaction monitoring procedures.

6.5.3 *Measurement of service quality*

The outcome of getting the service level right is profit. Profits for each regional office go into a worldwide pot for distribution among the partnership. This is an end result and obviously keenly watched by partners. Practice staffing levels are managed via the pyramid and the proportion of support to practice staff is carefully monitored.

At the individual staff level the primary report systems are the rating forms. Rating forms are simply a fact of life, 'you are rated as soon as you walk through the door', from how the staff dress and conduct their relationships with colleagues and clients to their technical skills.

Initially the rating process can be intimidating as the following quote from a partner illustrates:

> *It's such a vast organisation it's so determined to provide the best quality and that inevitably involves some sort of critical analysis of what you do. And to somebody who isn't quite used to that, which nobody is when they join the field – that can be quite intimidating. You get to live with it but the continuing evaluation by others of your work, means you are continually kept on your toes and that can be*

intimidating and a ruthless way of evaluating people ... as you come through the system you realise that people are only being honest.

The stress on client service is reinforced by the rating forms, as one partner explained:

We tell people all the time the focus is the client, we are about client service, our rating forms right down to assistant rating forms are on technical skills and client service. They know all the time that client service is of fundamental importance and they learn what aspects are going to be critical to their own advancement in the firm . We have had a number of people who are extremely gifted, who can put in beautiful work papers and can analyse any problem you want and there is no place for them in the long run. We do not keep career people, we are 'up or out' as an organisation and they can't go up because they cannot manage a client relationship, which is quite sad.

Although regular appraisal and counselling is provided there is a belief that nothing on the rating form should come as a shock to the individual being appraised. So, if there is a problem the policy is to inform the appraisee immediately, not wait until the next review. One partner described the importance of this in some detail:

It is important that people understand how they are perceived, not just that they are comfortable that they are doing as well as they hoped but if they are doing something wrong and you do not tell them quickly then they do not know how to address it. So a lot of the rating procedure and other performance procedures are there to make sure they know what is going on. One of the key controls is the rating form, when seniors learn how to fill them in they are told that nothing in there should come as a shock to the person who is being rated. So the idea is that as soon as you spot a problem or someone doing something particularly well, which we are not very good about telling them about, you discuss it with them so that they can address it then rather than a month later you get an appraisal which says you were rubbish at this. If you address it earlier people are not afraid that there is a hidden agenda because you are not getting feedback all of the time.

The formal process of rating is well understood and documented, though, some staff feel the 'informal perceptions are more important or fractionally more important than the formal rating structure'. There is a feeling that if you do particularly well on a job with a high-ranking manager that will tend to get on the grapevine.

6.5.4 *Rewards*

The high level of commitment to providing a quality service can place considerable pressure on individual members of staff. There is evidence of a strong 'team spirit' within the office. If a problem arises it will be dealt with, even if it is late in the day and someone else's client. Staff social activities are encouraged through corporate membership of a local gym and the tendency to go for a drink after work on Fridays, everyone is invited, partners, managers, secretaries although 'sometimes you are working such unsociable hours that the only people you have time to socialise with are the people you are working with ... you get to know them quite well.' There is an expectation that staff would, if needed, work extra hours, often at short notice, the pattern of work flow frequently being dictated by time differences in dealing with the USA, for example. This can be frustrating, as one secretary explained:

> *You have to work at Andersens to appreciate that you would be asked to stay to work until 10 at night when you are only a secretary. It's very hard to believe that you can be doing very little all day and then at 5 o'clock you have to go into overdrive ... we are paid overtime rates and if we work after 7 we are allowed travelling time and expenses, we get taxis home.*

The pressure and demands came as no surprise to the staff interviewed; the terms and conditions of the job had been made explicit from the outset. Financial rewards for working for Andersens are substantial, generally they pay above the going rate for new recruits; a generally expressed comment was 'twice the pay for three times the work'. It is acknowledged that 'you have to be committed 110 per cent to the company'. There are clear financial rewards in moving up the pyramid from assistant to partner and staff are under no illusions about their chances of reaching partnership. Staff who cannot manage the client relationship are the ones who leave.

> *A lot of our weeding out of people, is people that despite being very academically gifted may not be very good at building relationships with clients. So if you were to ask me one level down from that what builds those relationships I'm not sure I can tell you, its commercialism, some of it is having that common touch, not being a pure numbers person, not being an accountant ... we're accountants for non-accountants.*

The rating system is designed to encourage good performance and provides a mechanism for giving praise as well as identifying needs, this is clearly stated on the rating forms. However, the following quote from a manager summed up the staff view that partners tended not to praise:

> *I think it is fair to say that partners do not as a rule go out of their way to offer praise. So if you do get it that is simply seen as a gold star.*

This view was confirmed by one partner quoted above ' if (we) spot someone doing particularly well ... we are not very good at telling them about it .....'.

There are certain tangible areas of the job such as the general housekeeping, and completing the project on time within budget. One manager summed up the significant personal rewards in the following quote;

> *When you have given people good advice and they have acted on that advice and they are happy that you have saved them some tax or spotted an opportunity for them they are generally pleased with what you have done – that is quite a good feeling.*

6.6 *Conclusions*

Arthur Andersen is a large, worldwide partnership where all business is conducted in English; standard methodologies are used and quality of systems processes and people are guaranteed around the world. The firm has shown consistent growth. The critical mass coupled with the 'sharing culture' enables investments in developments such as the 'global best practice knowledge database', thus ensuring the 'best' most up to date advice is available to staff. Staff interviewed clearly felt that many firms used Andersens because it has a worldwide structure, they like the one firm concept, and the professional image presented by the organisation. The perception among staff is that Andersens is more expensive than many other firms but clients get good value for money; 'our audit approach is two to three years ahead of others'. Published fee income figures (*Accountancy*) show Andersens as having the highest fee/partner ratio and fees/professional staff ratio of the top fifty firms, however, it has a different business mix with a greater proportion of consultancy fees compared with other firms. External perceptions, in the UK, are of a very American and ruthless organisation whose staff work longer

hours than other firms. This is somewhat in conflict with the staff
support systems in place and the views of the staff interviewed.

6.6.1 *Does the performance measurement system support the corporate strategy?*

Internal perceptions indicate that the firm's strategy is well
understood throughout the organisation. Individuals demonstrate a
real pride in working for the organisation, they understand their
individual and collective responsibility for the reputation, style and
quality of the organisation and this is clearly motivating individual
performance.

The central question is whether the system of performance measures
captures the essence of Andersen's overall objectives of profitability,
growth and offering a high quality service. The answer is yes, as with
any service organisation the key people are the customer contact staff
and the focus of measurement must, necessarily, be based on those
staff. This process is aided by the clarity of communication of strategy
to all levels of staff. Everyone has a clear notion of the aims and
aspirations of the organisation and, perhaps more importantly, of their
individual roles in ensuring the corporate strategy is achieved. 'No
surprises' was a recurring phrase during the interviews, the idea being
that if you keep clients fully informed of issues/problems during the
process of a project, for example taking an aggressive stand on a tax
issue, the outcome should not come as a shock. The same 'no surprises'
philosophy underpins the staff reviewing process with the rating forms
giving regular feedback prior to the annual/six monthly reviews. There
was a feeling expressed by non-partner staff that while poor
performance is fully discussed, problem areas identified and solutions
offered, good performance is simply accepted. There was a clear desire
and need for the occasional 'well done', particularly from partners.

Arthur Andersen's success is clearly a function of both its size and the
quality of personnel employed. The firm has experienced
considerable expansion over the past ten years. The perception is
that many new partners were made in the boom years of the 1980s
and that 'making partner now is much more difficult'. This could
obviously affect morale. Some interviewees felt that the notion of
career managers and career seniors should be introduced. This would
challenge the fundamental character of the organisation and would
need careful management.

Review, Evaluation and Recommendations

'The best strategy is one which can actually be carried out! It is not a bit of good having a plan if there is no practicable way in which resistance to the concept can be overcome. … People work best when they know exactly what is expected of them, and that is just a little more than they themselves think they can achieve. This releases energy and poses a challenge.'

John Harvey-Jones, *Troubleshooter*,
BBC Books, 1990, pp 184-185

7.1 Introduction

The main focus of this research has been the detailed documentation and discussion of the performance measurement systems used within four successful service organisations. In this final chapter we draw out the similarities and differences across the four case studies using the framework of analysis introduced in Chapter 2. We summarise each performance measurement system in terms of the *dimensions* of performance measured (section 7.2), the way in which *standards* are set as targets to be attained on those dimensions (section 7.3), and the *reward* mechanisms that are adopted to encourage high performance levels (section 7.4).

In section 7.5 we summarise our research and suggest a series of general recommendations that represent best practice for the design of a performance measurement system. Following these general recommendations, we discuss how the specific characteristics of an organisation's system may vary according to service archetype (mass service, service shop or professional service). In the final section (section 7.6) we offer conclusions.

7.2 *Dimensions of performance*

Figure 7.1 summarises the main dimensions measured by the four organisations across four categories of performance indicator. Profit and competitiveness are the results of corporate success (or failure) while quality of service and resource utilisation are determinants of success.

All four companies adopt a wide range of performance measures, both financial and non-financial. All too have some focus on the bottom line; profit remains critically important. The difference is in the way this profit information is disclosed. The mass service (TNT) regularly publicises branch profits achieved via the use of league tables, making overall success or failure immediately transparent to other managers within the business. In contrast, knowledge of profits is restricted to the partners in the two professional organisations, and to dealership owners in the service shop.

At the company level where data is available about the market segment as a whole this is generally monitored on a formal basis; thus, for example, Arthur Andersen is well aware of its position (and movement in position) in the UK in terms of fee income. At the business unit level, however, only Peugeot formally measures its competitive performance using a published breakdown of new car registrations by postcode. The others use informal mechanisms; for example, Eversheds will gain knowledge of how it is doing, in comparison with its local competitors, through the careful cultivation of relationships with business providers such as banks and insurance companies.

Considerable effort is devoted to measuring service quality in all four organisations. There are clear distinctions between the approaches adopted in the professional services compared with the mass service, these largely result from the intrinsic nature of the business undertaken. Both Eversheds and Arthur Andersen review their performance with (almost) every client. Some facets of performance are relatively straightforward to measure, the winning of a legal case or the successful completion of an assignment in accordance with the original job specification; however, these are output measures. The nature of the client/professional service organisation relationship is that projects often last a considerable time with a high level of interaction between the client and staff. The challenge is to identify problems early during the process, so that corrective action can be

Figure 7.1: Dimensions of performance measured

	TNT	Peugeot	Eversheds	Arthur Andersen
Profit	By depot; publicised via league tables	By dealership	By office	By office and department
Competitiveness: *Market share at company level*	Informally	Published market research data	By relative size (i.e. no. of partners and fee earners)	Published UK fee income data
Market share at business unit level	Not measured	New car registrations by postcode	Informally through business providers (e.g. banks)	Informally through business providers
Quality of service: *On specific transactions*	Mystery customer, compliments files at head office	Mystery customer, post-transaction customer assessment	Case result, client evaluation interview	Client evaluation interview
Overall	7-star delivery performance league tables	Management inspections	Not measured	Not measured
Resource utilisation	Cost per consignment	Sales per employee, net profit per employee	Chargeable hours and chargeable fees per fee earner	Chargeable ratio, headcount

taken. This is achieved through some form of meeting, usually with the partner responsible, though the nature of the meeting will vary from client to client, with some wanting a formal interview type setting while others prefer a discussion over a pint in the pub. The driving force is 'no surprises'. If there are problems, then the earlier they are identified the quicker they can be rectified, there is no point in waiting until the end of the process to discover that there were problems.

In contrast, TNT has a large customer base with each transaction taking a relatively short time. Service quality on individual transactions is assessed on a sample basis using mystery shopper schemes. These are output measures and the results are used to drive continuous improvement. In addition, overall reports detailing service performance over a wide range of measures are produced weekly by depot, in a league table format.

The system at Peugeot is a hybrid of the approaches described above. Overall service performance is measured by management inspection, with individual transactions sampled in a mystery shopper system and every new car sale followed up with a customer assessment questionnaire. This assessment is repeated twelve and twenty-four months after initial purchase, which, as discussed earlier, is entirely consistent with trying to develop a long-term relationship with the customer.

All four organisations measure resource utilisation at the business unit level, but a further determinant of success, flexibility, is not formally monitored, although all the organisations have strategies for providing it. For example, Arthur Andersen are able to pull in resources from other offices, if necessary, because there are consistent standards throughout the organisation, while TNT will employ subcontractors to meet early deliveries if capacity constraints are broken.

Similarly, innovation is not formally measured by any of the four organisations. However, there is a recognition of the need to continually innovate, for example, Eversheds' policy of sending out formal letters of engagement on every job has been introduced relatively recently. The innovation process does not lend itself to monthly reporting, but it is an issue regularly debated at business planning meetings.

7.3 *Standards of performance*

The framework in Chapter 2 discussed three factors to consider in appraising the system used to set standards for the dimensions of performance.

- *Ownership* – do employees own their targets?
- *Achievability* – at what level are standards set?
- *Equity* – does the system cater for any variations between departments or branches that are outside the control of the employees?

Figure 7.2 summarises the standard-setting mechanisms used by the four companies across these three factors and distinguishes between standards set for profit and standards set for quality.

There was a clear distinction between the levels of ownership of profit targets and service quality targets. Managers participate in setting the profit targets – to greater degrees in the professional service companies – generally through the business planning process. In some cases there was clearly an overriding view on what level of business activity would be acceptable. At TNT, a manager at one of the more successful depots described the ever increasing targets as a 'fairy story'. In Peugeot, the negotiation is around sales targets rather than profit targets, a reflection of the franchise relationship between Peugeot and the dealership, with most of the dealerships being privately owned. Quality of service targets are almost invariably centrally driven, following the corporate viewpoint that a consistent level of quality should be apparent in any outlet of that business anywhere in the country. For TNT and Peugeot these measures are extensive and clearly defined. In the professional services the notion of service quality is more difficult to pinpoint. There is a clear view that a 'happy client' is important but breaking that measure down further is both difficult and probably of limited use, because different clients value different aspects of the service process.

Notwithstanding the TNT example referred to above, the profit and quality of service targets set are seen as being reasonably achievable. Within the two professional services, this partly reflects an acceptance of what is required of the job – 'as fee earners we need to attain a certain level of chargeable hours for the business to maintain its market position' – thus, the 'professionalism' of the fee earners leads to a positive attitude towards the targets. At the other two

Figure 7.2: Setting standards for performance

	TNT	Peugeot	Eversheds	Arthur Andersen
Ownership:				
Profit	Some involvement	Sales targets owned at dealership level	Set independently by office	Set independently by office
Quality of service	Centrally driven	Centrally driven	Centrally driven	Centrally driven
Achievability				
Profit	Increasingly difficult	Sales plan generally seen as achievable	Generally seen as achievable	Generally seen as achievable
Quality of service	Yes, via extensive internal benchmarking	Yes, via extensive internal benchmarking	Formal measures not set	Formal measures not set
Equity				
Profit	Allowance made for differences between depots regarding customer profile	Allowance made for territory in the sales plan	No allowance made for departmental differences in setting chargeable hours targets	Not applicable
Quality of service	No allowance made for locational disadvantages	No allowances made	Formal measures not set	Formal measures not set

organisations, TNT and Peugeot, the perceptions regarding achievability are driven by the extensive use of internal benchmarking. This creates 'irrefutable' evidence (according to management) that the targets are realistic; if one depot or store can achieve a certain level of performance in one area then there is no reason why other depots and stores elsewhere cannot do likewise. Thus, internal benchmarks are seen as important in the quest for continuous improvement, and hence in sustaining competitive edge. Externally determined benchmarks, which in some ways might be considered preferable, are also monitored where appropriate; for example, market share performance. However, at a detailed operations level, comparative information is generally not available, and so external benchmarking is rarely possible.

Internal benchmarking also has implications for the equity of the system. It creates absolute, though continually improving, standards for service quality, with the ultimate holy grail of perfect quality performance – 100 per cent on time deliveries, 100 per cent mystery shopper scores, or no late trunks to the hub. Formal allowance is not made for any systematic differences between specific sub-units. Thus, taking the latter example, the fine for a TNT lorry arriving late at the central sortation warehouse in Atherstone is the same whether it is travelling from Birmingham, 20 miles away, or Carlisle, 300 miles away. However, locational and other inbuilt differences are generally allowed for in setting profit targets. An exception is Eversheds where the target hours per fee earner remain the same regardless of the predicted effect of the economic climate on that fee earner's department. While litigation work may be fairly stable, property cases will fluctuate in accordance with the depth of the recession.

7.4 Reward mechanisms for achieving standards

In assessing the reward mechanisms used by organisations to encourage employees to achieve required levels of performance, there are three factors of importance.

- *Clarity* – do they understand what the company is trying to do?
- *Motivation* – what benefits, financial or otherwise, will they gain for achieving their targets?
- *Controllability* – are they assessed only on those factors they can control?

Figure 7.3: Reward mechanisms adopted

	TNT	Peugeot	Eversheds	Arthur Andersen
Clarity	All employees very aware of the 'need to get the service level right'	High awareness of Peugeot strategy at dealer level	Required standards of professionalism and service quality well understood though not explicitly stated	Required standards of professionalism and service quality stressed through extensive staff appraisal forms
Motivation *Financial (short-term)*	Extensive rewards mechanisms at all levels	Significant bonus on quality of dealership service	Partners' earnings dependent on office profits: no fee earner bonus scheme but pay rise linked to staff appraisal	Partners' earnings dependent on world profits: no fee earner bonus scheme but pay rise linked to staff appraisal
Non-financial	Pride in league table performance	Working in the business (a 'love of cars'); profit clinics as support mechanisms	Prospect of making partner; respectable firm; good working environment	Prospect of making partner; working for the 'No. 1' worldwide accounting firm; high-quality training
Controllability	Non-matching of costs and revenues on consignments; full allocation of head office 'group service' costs to depots	No control over the product range – tied to Peugeot through franchise agreement	No controllability issues highlighted	Central costs allocated to departments

In Figure 7.3 the four organisations' performance measurement systems are summarised across these three factors.

One feature that stands out from our research is that in all case organisations employees interviewed exhibited a high awareness of the essential ingredients of their organisation's corporate strategy, and its implications regarding their own performance. Almost everybody interviewed at TNT emphasised the need to 'get the service level right', while at Arthur Andersen employees are left with little doubt as to the key characteristics necessary for a successful career path, given the comprehensive nature of the staff assessment procedures after every assignment undertaken.

In terms of motivation, it is perhaps not surprising that there is a noticeable pride in working for the company, as all are very successful organisations within their industrial segment. Arthur Andersen, for instance, is one of the top accounting and consultancy firms in the world, a fact that somehow adds to employees' self esteem. At Peugeot, there is also an evident pride in the product being sold, employees openly demonstrating a real love and enthusiasm for cars.

More concrete incentives are provided by monetary bonus schemes linked to performance. At TNT and Peugeot this is transparent with clear linkages between the performance level achieved and the amount of the bonus. At Eversheds and Arthur Andersen there is no bonus scheme, though it is acknowledged that a staff member's annual pay review is based in part on an assessment of their job performance. For these professional services the main incentive is undoubtedly the long-term prospect of making it to partner. Partners themselves, of course, have a direct financial stake in the business; their income depending on the profitability of the firm.

The controllability principle suggests that the performance of people should only be measured and rewarded on the basis of factors within their domain of control. Across the four organisations investigated the most striking departure from this concept was at TNT. Here, while several parties are actually involved in the service process for a particular package, only one depot receives the benefit of the revenue generated. Income is credited to the collecting depot, where the sale originated, rather than being allocated between the collecting and delivering depots, and possibly the hub as well. At times this results in some frustrations at the delivery depots, though there is an acknowledgement that for many (though not all) depots things balance out in the long run. The dual advantages of this method are its simplicity and its reinforcement of the teamwork ethic, important in a network organisation.

7.5 *Performance measurement system recommendations*

It is clear from the above comparisons that there are both similarities and differences in the way in which the organisations studied have designed their performance measurement systems. There is no single set of performance measures, no single basis for setting standards for those measures, and no universal reward mechanism that constitute some perfect performance measurement system applicable in all contexts. However, emerging from this research are several themes which, together, represent common characteristics of the measurement systems adopted. We suggest that these serve as necessary preconditions for the attainment of best practice.

1. *Know what you are trying to do*

The starting point is to clearly articulate the overall corporate strategy of the organisation and then to identify those factors that are critical to its success. That is, the design of the performance measurement system must be rooted in an understanding of exactly what the organisation needs to do to exploit its sources of competitive advantage. This understanding should also be communicated throughout the organisation, so that all employees are aware of the company goals towards which they are working. In all four case organisations employees exhibited a clear understanding of their organisation's corporate objectives and image, particularly with regard to quality of service.

2. *Adopt a range of measures*

It is well understood that the traditional catch-all financial measures such as return-on-investment are inadequate for capturing the complexity of modern business operations. Organisations should adopt a range of measures covering six generic dimensions of performance; financial performance, competitiveness, quality, resource utilisation, flexibility and innovation. The performance measures used are likely to include financial and non-financial indicators, but should focus on the critical success factors identified above. In addition, the adoption of a range of measures helps to alleviate the potential problems of dysfunctional behaviour, notorious where managers' performance is captured through a single measure. Within each generic dimension of performance the number and range of indicators adopted will be highly variable depending on the nature of the organisation and its market position. At the Peugeot motor dealership network, for instance, the Lion Standards programme involves the evaluation of 71 separate factors within the operating standards component, just one of three components in the overall quality programme.

3. Extract comparative measures to assess performance outcomes

It is not always obvious what constitutes a successful outcome. Thus, performance measures need to be assessed against some standard. One possibility is to define the standards on the basis of internal benchmarking, so that the performance achievements of the 'best' units become the targets for all other outlets, leading to a culture of continuous improvement. As an alternative or as a supplement to this absolute performance comparison, relative comparisons can be made by directly displaying the results of all outlets in the form of published league tables. This use of league tables was noticeably widespread in the case of the mass service, TNT, where depots' relative performance is summarised weekly for profits and delivery, and monthly for finance and administration.

4. Report results regularly

For managers to be able to use the performance information proactively, it must be relevant and up-to-date. Organisations should be disciplined in reporting key performance measures on a regular basis. In the mass service and the service shop organisations investigated, key results are reported monthly and in some cases weekly, while Arthur Andersen produce reports after every job. This formal reporting mechanism leads to a large amount of information being produced but enables a faster reaction time in reproducing improvements and alleviating problems.

5. Drive the system down from the top

Finally, but equally importantly, it is imperative that managers throughout the organisation believe in the performance measurement system as representing a worthwhile use of their time and resources. This will largely be an exercise in corporate communication, but is likely to be most successful if there is a strong, well-respected corporate champion driving the system down from the top, who uses the resultant performance outcomes as a basis for regular dialogue between unit managers and the corporate management team. The successful design and implementation of the performance measurement systems at TNT is due, to a large extent, to the depth of investment made in them by the managing director.

For a performance measurement system to be an effective management tool, these five characteristics should, in our view, be key ingredients within *any* organisation. They represent, though, general characteristics, rather than a menu of specific performance indicators. The precise specification of a system will be contingent on many factors; for example, whether the organisation is predominantly manufacturing or service; the type of product(s) and production processes; the number of outlets; the degree of importance attached to the performance measurement system by senior management; and the ease of data measurement.

In Chapter 2, we discussed the three different service archetypes – mass service, service shop, and professional service. In addition to the contingent factors above, how then does this further factor of service archetype impact on performance measurement choice? Our research reveals that it appears to make no systematic difference. Turnover and profit are measured in standard ways, budgetary control systems are essentially very similar, and reward packages in the four organisations all display some combination of financial and non-financial mechanisms.

However, the one key area where service archetype appears to make a difference to the performance measurement system is in the measurement of service quality. The mass service (TNT) and the service shop (Peugeot) both monitor overall service quality through regularly published operations performance statistics. For the most part, this comprises detailed, hard, objective data such as the number of on-time deliveries or the number of late trunks to the hub. However, because of the high volume of transactions passing through the system, at the level of an individual transaction it is necessary to monitor quality on a sample basis. Thus, both TNT and Peugeot employ mystery shoppers to assess the quality and reliability of the service process. In contrast, the two professional services (Eversheds and Arthur Andersen) monitor service quality on virtually every transaction, usually through a client evaluation interview on completion of the assignment; that is, by adopting softer, more subjective performance indicators. The interview might be short or long, formal or informal, but whatever its format the firms will gain direct feedback as to the customer's perceptions of their service quality.

7.6 *Conclusions*

This book has described in some detail the performance measurement systems adopted within four successful UK service organisations. A comparison of the organisations has been made using a framework of analysis, developed in Chapter 2, that addresses three sets of questions: what *dimensions* of performance are measured, how are appropriate *standards* set, and what *rewards* are associated with achieving the targets? These are the building blocks for performance measurement.

Our view is that there is no single set of performance measures, no single basis for setting standards for those measures and no universal reward mechanism that constitute some perfect performance measurement system applicable in all contexts. Generic dimensions of performance such as financial performance, competitiveness, quality and resource utilisation should all be measured. The translation of these generic dimensions into a set of performance measures will be a function of the competitive strategy being adopted and the type of service being delivered. Setting targets for performance will continue to be an area of lively debate. In our sample organisations, internal benchmarking is used extensively to defuse this argument, with the overriding message that there will be no compromise on quality targets. Rewards for achievement vary from tangible monthly financial bonuses to the more intangible 'feel good' factor because someone – a customer or a colleague – says 'well done'.

All of the companies were actively using their performance measurement systems to translate strategy into action. The systems and measures used were under constant review and had been changed, and will continue to change over time, as the focus of strategy changes. We recognise that the performance measurement systems reported here represent snapshots taken at a specific period of time in the organisations' histories and that in the search for continuous improvement some of those detailed measures may have changed. Nevertheless, what emerges from our research is a set of five common characteristics which we suggest are essential prerequisites for the attainment of best practice in the development of a performance measurement system:

- *Know what you are trying to do* – this must be driven by the corporate strategy.
- *Adopt a range of measures* – financial and non-financial.
- *Extract comparative measures* – there must be a benchmark for performance.
- *Report results regularly* – this discipline promotes knowledge and action.
- *Drive the system from the top* – senior management need to use the system.